AF352282

OT

534238

Isaiah xxi
A palimpsest

Isaiah xxi

A palimpsest

A. A. MACINTOSH

Fellow, Tutor and Dean of St John's College, Cambridge

CAMBRIDGE UNIVERSITY PRESS

Cambridge

London   New York   New Rochelle
Melbourne   Sydney

Published by the Press Syndicate of the University of Cambridge
The Pitt Building, Trumpington Street, Cambridge CB2 1RP
32 East 57th Street, New York, NY 10022, USA
296 Beaconsfield Parade, Middle Park, Melbourne 3206, Australia

© Cambridge University Press 1980

First published 1980

Printed in Great Britain at the
University Press, Cambridge

British Library Cataloguing in Publication Data
Macintosh, Andrew Alexander
Isaiah XXI.
1. Bible. Old Testament. Isaiah XXI – Criticism,
interpretation, etc.
I. Title II. Bible. Old Testament. Isaiah XXI.
English. 1980
224'.1   BS1515.2   79–41375
ISBN 0 521 22943 X

*To my wife and to all others
who have cheered on the tow-path*

Contents

Acknowledgements

I wish to record my gratitude to the trustees of the Bethune-Baker Fund of the University of Cambridge for a generous grant to assist in the publication of this work; to J. A. Emerton, Regius Professor of Hebrew in the University of Cambridge and a colleague in the fellowship of St John's College, who read earlier drafts and made many helpful suggestions; to Valerie Collis for her generous and enthusiastic help with typing and indexing; to N. C. Buck and M. B. Pratt of St John's College Library for their unfailing helpfulness; to Cambridge University Press (and particularly to R. Coleman and Jane Van Tassel) for their patient care of my work.

A.A.M.

St John's College
27 December 1979

Principal abbreviations

A.N.E.T.	J. B. Pritchard, *Ancient Near Eastern Texts Relating to the Old Testament* (Princeton, N.J., 1950)
B.A.S.O.R.	*Bulletin of the American Schools of Oriental Research*
B.D.B.	F. Brown, S. R. Driver and C. A. Briggs, *A Hebrew and English Lexicon of the Old Testament* (Oxford, 1907)
B.H.[(3)]	*Biblia Hebraica*, 3rd edn, ed. R. Kittel (Stuttgart, 1937)
B.H.S.	*Biblia Hebraica Stuttgartensia*, ed. D. W. Thomas (Stuttgart, 1968)
C.A.H.	*The Cambridge Ancient History*. See Principal Works Consulted, sect. 7
D.K.	C. F. A. Dillmann and R. Kittel, *Der Prophet Jesaja*, 6th edn (Leipzig, 1898)
E.T.	English translation
G.K.	Gesenius–Kautzsch, *Gesenius' Hebrew Grammar*, 2nd English edn, rev. A. E. Cowley (Oxford, 1910)
H.U.C.A.	*Hebrew Union College Annual*
J.A.O.S.	*Journal of the American Oriental Society*
J.B.L.	*Journal of Biblical Literature*
J.N.E.S.	*Journal of Near Eastern Studies*
J.R.A.S.	*Journal of the Royal Asiatic Society*
J.S.S.	*Journal of Semitic Studies*
J.T.S.	*Journal of Theological Studies*
K.B.	L. Koehler and W. Baumgartner, *Lexicon in Veteris Testamenti Libros* (Leiden, 1953)
K.B.[(3)]	L. Koehler and W. Baumgartner, *Hebräisches und Aramäisches Lexikon zum Alten Testament*, 3rd edn, ed. W. Baumgartner, B. Hartmann and E. Y. Kutscher, vols. I–II (Leiden, 1967–74)
LXX	The Septuagint. See Principal Works Consulted, sect. 2

M.T.	The Massoretic Text. See Principal Works Consulted, sect. 1
N.E.B.	The New English Bible
P.E.Q.	*Palestine Exploration Quarterly*
P.T.	The Palestinian Talmud. See Principal Works Consulted, sect. 7 (Talmud)
1QIs^a	The (complete) Isaiah Scroll from Qumran cave 1. For the text, see M. Burrows (ed.), *The Dead Sea Scrolls of St. Mark's Monastery,* vol. 1 (New Haven, Conn., 1950)
R.B.	*Revue Biblique*
R.E.J.	*Revue des Etudes Juives*
R.S.V.	The Revised Standard Version of the Bible
R.V.	The Revised Version of the Bible
Th.St.Kr.	*Theologische Studien und Kritiken*
V.T.	*Vetus Testamentum*
W.O.	*Die Welt des Orients*
Z.A.W.	*Zeitschrift für die Alttestamentliche Wissenschaft*
Z.D.M.G.	*Zeitschrift der Deutschen Morgenländischen Gesellschaft*
Z.Th.K.	*Zeitschrift für Theologie und Kirche*

Introduction

Any attempt to interpret and to understand prophetical texts of the O.T. must take into account a number of factors which are so closely related to each other that it is difficult to determine their order of priority. The factors include: an estimate of the likely historical background of the text, the recognition of the literary forms which the prophet uses, the establishing of the exact meaning of his words and expressions, and the sifting of those words and expressions so as to recognize any secondary interpretations and additions either by the prophet or by those who transmitted his words.

It may seem correct to attempt first to establish the text and the meaning of its words and expressions. Yet considerable difficulties arise in the case of texts in which many words and phrases are ambiguous or obscure. For the attempt to resolve problems of meaning depends to some extent upon an estimate of the attitude of the prophet and of what he is likely to have said or to have written in a particular historical situation. Thus, if the prophet of Isa. xxi is, like that of Isa. xiii, concerned with the imminent fall of the Babylonian empire in 539 B.C., then it is possible that he gave expression in xxi 2 to the sentiment: 'Cause all her [*sc.* Babylon's] pride to cease';[1] for such sentiments were indeed expressed by prophets as they contemplated that fall (e.g. Isa. xiii 19). But from the philological point of view, 'pride' is but one possibility amongst several for the word אנחתה[2] and a different understanding of the historical background of the prophecy may at once render 'pride' unlikely and another possibility (on that assumption) probable.

Alternatively, it may seem appropriate from a preliminary

---

1 So Eitan; see below. (For all citations by author alone, see Principal Works Consulted, pp. 144–50.)

2 And some of these are equally suitable to the circumstances of the fall of Babylon in 539 B.C.

study of the text to estimate what is its historical background and thereafter to interpret all the words and phrases of the text in the light of that estimate. Yet this procedure too may lead the interpreter astray: first, it may blind him to the possibility that the words of the text have been reinterpreted and redirected by those who transmitted them to situations and circumstances different from those in which originally they were uttered by the prophet himself; and, secondly, it may lead the commentator to overinterpret the text, to find detailed historical references where none exists. For, as it is generally agreed, prophets were not interested primarily in the events of history but in the interpretation of those events, and what they have given us are not purely historical records but religious pronouncements (cf. Otzen, pp. 36f).

What I have said of the relationship between estimates of the likely historical background and the meaning of the text is true also of the relationship between the meaning of the text and the literary forms employed by the prophets. For from the understanding of the words of the text is derived recognition of literary forms, and yet recognition of literary forms effects the illumination of words and phrases of the text. Thus, the obscure words and dialectal forms of the Dumah oracle (Isa. xxi 11f), by virtue of the words and forms that are apparently not obscure and dialectal, may be interpreted as appropriate to a watchman's dialogue with those who by night await entry to his city gate. In the light of that supposition an estimate is given of the meaning of the obscure words and phrases (so Lohmann; see below).

So to determine the context in which words are given precise meanings is, however, far from certainly reliable, as is clear from the existence of other treatments of the easier words of the Dumah oracle; for such alternative treatments in turn give rise to other estimates of the context and consequently to different meanings being given to the difficult words.

The recognition of such difficulties and the fact that they attend all attempts at interpreting prophetical texts serve as a warning to interpreters that guesswork and supposition form an integral part of their task and that consequently no interpretation is likely to be finally correct. Rather the grounds upon which our guesses and estimates are made must be continually reviewed in the light of the increase in our knowledge of ancient Near Eastern history as well as of the language and literature of the Old Testament.

The purpose of the present study is to conduct such a review in regard to Isa. xxi. To that end the text and language of the chapter will first be examined; the meaning of its words and phrases will be discussed in the light of interpretations of them made by the ancient versions, by medieval Jewish scholars and by modern commentators. In the light of this examination, consideration will be given to the historical background of the oracles of the chapter, their literary forms and their interpretation in the tradition of the bible itself as well as in later times.

I

The Text and Its Meaning: A Preliminary Survey

Verses 1–10

Verse 1a, מַשָּׂא מִדְבַּר־יָם

The words are generally taken to be the title of the prophecy contained in verses 1–10. As is clearly the case in Isa. xxi 13 and in Isa. xxii 1 (cf. xxx 6), the title is derived from a keyword contained within the oracle itself. The main verb בא of this verse is followed immediately by the word ממדבר and it is this that was regarded as the keyword. All witnesses to the M.T. substantiate the reading מדבר ים except 1QIs[a] which reads דבר for מדבר and the LXX which, with τὸ ὅραμα τῆς ἐρήμου, appears to have read simply מדבר.[1]

By analogy with the other texts cited and on the evidence of the LXX, it may be presumed that משא (מ)מדבר is an older reading[2] and that the later reading מדבר ים (of which 1QIs[a]'s דבר ים is perhaps a corruption) arose either as a deliberate expansion of the original title or from a corruption of a word originally occurring as the first word of the main text of the oracle;[3] in either event the change gave the title a different significance from that of its earlier form.

If משא (מ)מדבר is indeed the original form of the title, then being a mere repetition of the word (מ)מדבר contained in the

---

1 For the view that the text of the LXX originally included the word θαλάσσης and that the word was subsequently omitted by a scribe who did not understand its meaning, see Rosenmüller.

2 It is possible that the preposition (מ)ן was originally prefixed to the word מדבר in the title (as it is in the text of the oracle) in the same way as ב occurs prefixed to the word ערב in the title of verse 13 as well as in the text. The Targum, quoted below, employs the preposition מן. On this view the first מ may have dropped out by haplography and the resulting מדבר was thought to be in need of an explanatory gloss; cf. Kaiser. On the other hand, the ב prefixed to ניא חזין (xxii 5) is not found in the title of xxii 1.

3 So Cobb, Marti, Scott and G. R. Driver; for their views, see pp. 8ff.

4

text, no further interpretation of the words is necessary. But the reading משא מדבר ים, however it arose, is clearly early and must be intended to furnish, or was seen to furnish, a title suitable to the contents of the prophecy over which it stands.

As the prophecy with which we are concerned culminates (verse 9) with the dramatic cry 'Babylon is fallen', it has long been customary to see in the title מדבר ים a reference to that city. Thus, Theodoret (c. 393–c. 458, Bishop of Cyrus in Syria), comments: ἔρημον θάλασσαν τὴν βαβυλῶνα καλεῖ.[1] Similarly, ibn Ezra and Qimhi, for whom the prophecy as a whole concerns the fall of Babylon in 539 B.C. at the hands of the Medes and Persians, suggest that Babylon is called מדבר ים because it lies to the west of the Medes and Persians and because the word ים is capable of that meaning (cf. B.D.B., p. 411a). For ibn Ezra it is called מדבר by prolepsis (i.e. Babylon is soon to become a desert), though in Qimhi's opinion מדבר is used in order to indicate that the territory which lies between Persia and Babylon, and over which the imminent invasion is to come, is desert.

In fact, these comments are less appropriate to the title מדבר ים than to the phrase ממדבר בא within the prophecy itself, for they are concerned not so much with Babylon as with the mode and direction of the attack upon it. It may be suggested that Qimhi's comment at least has been influenced by the interpretation of the Targum (which he quotes): מטלן משרין דאתין מן מדברא 'The oracle (or *march*) of the armies which come from the wilderness', and that this interpretation in turn is ultimately derived from the words ממדבר בא within the oracle itself, whether or not the Targum actually read in the title (as is possible) ממדבר (i.e. with preposition).[2]

Amongst modern scholars, Dillmann–Kittel and Fohrer follow these rabbinic commentators in the sense that they regard the phrase as indicating not Babylon but the desert of South Babylonia which lies on the Persian Gulf either south-east of Babylon between the city and Elam (D.K.), or west of the lower Euphrates (Fohrer); consequently the phrase indicates the direction of the attack on the city. This interpretation of the title (which both scholars regard as a later addition) may be

1 For the text, see Möhle.
2 That the Targum also read ים is clear from the next phrase in it: כמי ימא.

regarded as plausible only if the contents of verse 1 do in fact refer to armies advancing on Babylon from the desert. But that view rests upon an interpretation of verse 1 which is far from certain.

Other geographical allusions to Babylon or its environs are seen by modern scholars. Thus Delitzsch[1] considers that מדבר denotes the great plain on which Babylon stood and which in the south was so intersected by marshes and lakes, as well as by the Euphrates, that it floated, as it were, in the sea and indeed was called θάλασσα by Abydenus (*apud* Eusebius, *Praeparatio Evangelica* ix 41). Further, such natural features of Babylon are taken by the prophet, fond as he is of symbolical names, to refer to its ultimate fate. Thus, Jeremiah (li 13), who according to Delitzsch (1) knew this oracle, 'was acquainted with its true significance'.

Secondly, attention is drawn to the Akkadian phrase *māt tâmti* 'the land of the sea' (see Schrader, p. 353) used by the Assyrians to describe South Babylonia (i.e. the land nearest the Persian Gulf) and it is suggested that מדבר ים is the Hebrew equivalent of it.[2] Against this view, however, may be set the arguments advanced by Dillmann–Kittel: if South Babylonia is called Θάλασσα/*māt tâmti* then it is unlikely that upper Babylonia and the city itself should be so called. Further, that מדבר ים is a Hebrew equivalent of *māt tâmti* is far from clear; for why should *māt* 'land' be translated 'desert'? Dhorme's argument that the presumably accurate equivalent ארץ ים would have given rise to a bald contradiction in terms and that it was therefore modified to מדבר ים 'steppe of the sea' is scarcely convincing, for even if it does not merely replace one contradiction in terms by another, the word מדבר is not elsewhere used to denote tracts of land covered with lakes and marshes.[3]

---

1 His views appear to be dependent upon a number of earlier scholars; see Michaelis and Vitringa.

2 So Cheyne, *P.I.*, and more recently P. Dhorme in *R.B.* 31 (1922), pp. 403ff, followed by Erlandsson.

3 Dhorme, followed tentatively by Erlandsson, further suggests that there is in the title מדבר ים a deliberate reference to *māt tâmti*, Merodach-baladan's abode in South Babylonia which was also called *Bīt Yakin* (Merodach-baladan was called 'son of Yakin'). Apart from the fact that the suggestion rests on a number of questionable textual assumptions (as has been shown above), it is also unlikely on the grounds that no further reference to South Babylonia is discernible in the prophecy.

In conclusion, I accept the view that the original title of the oracle read מַשָּׂא מ(ד)בר[1] and that the later reading משא מדבר ים has been subsequently interpreted in one way or another as being an appropriate reference to some aspect of the contents of the prophecy.

Verse 1b, כְּסוּפוֹת בַּנֶּגֶב לַחֲלוֹף מִמִּדְבָּר בָּא מֵאֶרֶץ נוֹרָאָה

The sentence appears to consist of a main verb (בא), apparently without an expressed subject. Whoever or whatever 'comes' (or 'has come')[2] does so from the desert (ממדבר) which is further defined as a 'terrible land' (ארץ נוראה).[3] The manner of his or its coming is described by a simile, כספות בנגב לחלוף 'like whirlwinds sweeping along in the Negeb'.

The ancient versions witness to a text which differs little (if at all) from the M.T., though the LXX and Peshitta appear to have understood the whirlwind as a singular (ὡς καταιγìς/ʾyk ʿlʿlʾ) and to have divided the phrases of the sentence rather differently. The LXX's feminine ἐρχομένη (cf. Pesh.: wtʾtʾ), which corresponds to the M.T.'s בא, may be held to indicate that this version (so the Pesh.)[4] took the whirlwind to be the subject of בא as well as of the gerundial infinitive construct לחלף. The Targum, with כמי ימא דנגדין ('like the waters of the sea which sweep along'), appears to have interpreted the ים of the M.T.'s title as part of the simile;[5] its main verb ואתן which answers to the M.T.'s בא is predicated of the armies (משרין) which it has supplied as a subject.

The Targum's interpretation of the main verb בא, viz. that an invading army must be understood as its subject, is followed by ibn Ezra and Qimhi (cf. Rashi) who again refer to the expedition of Medes and Persians against Babylon which arrives from the desert between the city and Persian Sea. The inter-

---

1 So, essentially, Duhm, Marti, Gray, Procksch, Kaiser, Wildberger, etc.

2 So Wildberger, on the grounds that הִגַּד in the following verse is perfect.

3 On the 'terrible land', see further below.

4 In the case of the Peshitta, it is not immediately clear what is the subject of the feminine verb(s). However, the noun ʿlʿlʾ is the only feminine noun in the verse, and for this reason the judgement is made that, as in the LXX, the whirlwind is the subject.

5 Though not to the exclusion of the whirlwinds which are also included in the strange phrase כמי ימא דנגדין בעלעולין אתן 'like the waters of the sea which sweep along in whirlwinds do they (sc. the armies) come'.

pretation is adopted by a number of modern commentators, and, like the Targum, they seem to assume it from the context (see Rosenmüller; Delitzsch; Cheyne, *P.I.*; D.K., and Kaiser).

Amongst the rabbinic commentators, Saadya alone does not follow the interpretation of the Targum. The words ממדבר בא are rendered by him (in Arabic) אמר כאלזואבע…יאתי מן אלברֿ ('Un événement, semblable aux tourbillons…arrivera du desert').

It may be assumed that he wished to reproduce more literally the sense of the M.T. with its unexpressed subject, though it is interesting to note that in his translation he appears to feel the need to supply some indication of how the verb is to be under-stood. From what follows in verse 2 of his translation, viz. that the inhabitants of the terrible land say that they have been told a hard prophecy, it appears that he understands (the news of) the terrible event (אמר) to be the subject of the verb בא. In any case this is an alternative explanation of the verb בא which is adopted by those moderns who, like Saadya, do not follow the Targum's understanding of it (so e.g. Duhm, Gray, Marti and Procksch). For them the (unexpressed) subject of בא is under-stood as the terrible import of the vision described in verse 2, later (verse 9) precisely defined as the fall of Babylon. For these commentators the desert from which the news comes is the Syrian desert which lies between Babylon and the (Palestinian) dwelling place of the prophet.

As I have observed in my comments on the (M.T.) title of the oracle, some modern scholars have seen in ים a corruption of the initial word of this prophecy. In part, attempts to restore this supposed first word are designed also to alleviate the problem of the unexpressed subject of the verb בא. Marti[1] suggests that ים is a corruption of an original הֶמְיָה 'a roaring as of storms which sweep on in the Negeb! It comes etc.' By making the simile clearly attach to the word המיה he frees בא to be read more closely with what follows in verse 2. The construction, however, remains somewhat awkward and the emendation purely conjectural.

Secondly, R. B. Y. Scott,[2] on the basis of the reading of

1 He rightly rejects Cobb's earlier suggestion that ים is the perfect of a lost ימם with the same sense.
2 In *V.T.* 2 (1952), 278ff.

1QIs[a], suggests that the beginning of verse 1 is corrupted by haplography from an original משא מדבר דברים כסופות etc. and he suggests that the main verb בא was originally בָּאִים. The meaning of the text of the oracle so restored is: 'Words are coming like storm winds which sweep on in the Negeb.' Against such a restoration and consequent emendation of the text are the telling arguments of Kaiser, who urges that בא when predicated of דבר means 'fulfil, come to pass' and never denotes the initial reception of a revelation.

More plausible is the solution proposed by G. R. Driver[1] and adopted by the N.E.B. For Driver ים is read יֹם (יוֹם) and taken to mean '(stormy) weather' after the meaning 'stormy weather, storm demon' attested for the Accadian cognate word *ūmu*. Driver suggests that the word יום bears this meaning also in Judg. xix 11, and it may be noted that K.B.[(3)] (p. 384) suggest the similar meaning 'wind' for יום in Song of Songs ii 17 and iv 6[2] and 'storms' in Zeph. ii 2.[3] The translation offered by Driver runs: '(Stormy) weather, like tempests in the South in their passing, comes from the wilderness, from a terrible land.'[4]

Driver's treatment and interpretation of the text have the great merit that they furnish בא with a subject and afford a clear and straightforward construction for the verse which as a whole becomes a simile or parable. For Driver the parable alludes to the westward sweep of the Elamites and Medes whose armies come across the intervening desert to overrun Babylon.

However, it is more natural to suppose that the storm is a parable of (or is coincident with) the coming to the prophet of his 'harsh vision'[5] (verse 2) rather than of invading armies. For while the desert is not further defined in the prophecy, the simile within the verse itself ('like whirlwinds') refers to the

---

1 P. 46.
2 For a different view, see W. Rudolph, *K.A.T.* xvii, following D. W. Thomas in *Expository Times* 47 (1935–6), 431f.
3 It is not possible here to examine in detail the theory of Driver and Baumgartner other than in relation to Isa. xxi 1. It is possible to argue, however, that the usual translation 'day' makes good sense in Judg. xix 11 and Zeph. ii 2 and that it is possible in the passages from Song of Songs.
4 Procksch, commenting on בא, similarly suggested that what comes is the (ghostly) storm; for him, however, that meaning is discernible by carrying over the sense of an initial יְהֶמה (sic, after Marti).
5 So, with a different understanding of the text, Marti, Procksch, Gray, Duhm.

Negeb, i.e. the desert of southern Palestine,[1] a place of sudden swift-moving storms (cf. Ps. xxix) which are alluded to elsewhere in the O.T. as a symbol of Yahweh's impending intervention in the affairs of his people (Judg. v 4, Hab. iii 3, Zech. ix 14). On this view, the imagery of the verse indicates that Yahweh has revealed to the prophet his 'harsh vision' (verse 2), and that he is the author of the awesome events which are proclaimed by it.[2]

ארץ נוראה 'a terrible land'. The phrase is most likely to be construed as in apposition to מדבר and as referring to the same desert; cf. Deut. i 19 and viii 15 (so Rashi).

In 1QIs[a] נוראה is found superimposed upon the word רחוקה which has been deleted. The Peshitta, too, implies the reading רחוקה (*ʾrꜥ rhyqtʾ*) and these facts suggest a textual tradition at variance with the M.T. If this is the case then memory of it may have survived also to the time of Qimhi who, commenting on ארץ נוראה, states that the land of the Medes and Persians is meant 'for they are far from Babylon'. He continues: הרחוק יקרא נורא לפי שהאדם ירא הרחוק 'the far-off is terrible because men fear it'.

On the other hand, the evidence of 1QIs[a] and of the Peshitta may be taken to indicate a very early interpretation of נוראה which subsequently found its way into some textual traditions. If the form-critical observations on the prophecy set out below (chapter 3) are correct, then the word רחוקה is a later interpretation of the word נוראה.

The Targum interprets the phrase מארעא דאתעבידא בה חסינן 'from the land where terrible things are wrought' and this too may reflect the interpretation of the 'terrible land' as that of the Medes and Persians. Certainly ibn Ezra and Qimhi (the latter quoting the Targum) take this view.[3]

לחלף. For an infinitive construct with לְ to describe attendant circumstances or to define more precisely, see G.K. 114o. The word depicts 'the swift passage of the storms' (Driver).

1　The argument that נגב here means the (Arabian) desert south of Babylon (Delitzsch followed by D.K.) is most unlikely, for the word נגב is not elsewhere attested as referring to any other specific geographical area than that to the south of Judah.

2　Wildberger similarly finds such an allusion in the phrase.

3　They are followed by Delitzsch, and tentatively by D.K. For Duhm, Babylon, the scene of terrifying events, is meant.

Verse 2a, חָזוּת קָשָׁה הֻגַּד לִי

The verse begins with the phrase 'A grievous (or hard) vision is declared to me' (R.V.).

The fact that the passive verb is third person masculine singular and that חזות is feminine suggests that the construction is that described in G.K. 121a–b; the passive is used impersonally with the object of the active construction still subordinated in the accusative, i.e. 'There is/was told to me a harsh vision' (cf. Gen. xxvii 42). Saadya's קד אלכברנא בנבא צעב 'we have been informed of a harsh vision' is grammatically accurate.[1]

קָשָׁה, 'harsh' or 'calamitous'; cf. with Cheyne 1 Kings xiv 6. The problems of the passage in which the phrase occurs are largely exegetical and must be considered later in regard to the whole form of the oracle. Here it may be observed that, on the whole, rabbinic commentators considered that the vision was harsh specifically for Babylon (ibn Ezra, Rashi, Qimhi), though they follow the Targum in interpreting לי as referring to the prophet himself. Saadya, however, understands לי as referring to the inhabitants of the terrible land (אהלה יקול) 'its inhabitants say...', which suggests that he understood the phrase as a quotation. Dillmann-Kittel and Gray consider it significant that the vision is heard rather than seen by the prophet, and they refer to verse 6 where a watchman relates to the prophet what he has seen (i.e. the watchman sees, and the prophet hears).

Verse 2b, הַבּוֹגֵד בּוֹגֵד וְהַשּׁוֹדֵד שׁוֹדֵד

The four words evidently characterize in an epigrammatical way the contents of the harsh vision.

בגד. The word is generally taken to denote treacherous conduct,[2] specifically in matters of property and rights (e.g. Ex. xxi 8), in regard to adultery (e.g. Jer. iii 20), to disobedience (1 Sam. xiv 33), to broken trust (Job vi 15) and to rebellion (Judg. ix 23).[3] Rosenmüller suggests the meaning 'plunder' for this word because the parallelism demands it and because, he says,

---

1 Qimhi assumes that the passive verb implies the agency of God.
2 See B.D.B., K.B.[(3)] and Gesenius–Buhl.
3 Michaelis's view that 'contempt' is an older meaning of the word does not affect its usage in the present text.

the verb is very often translated by Aramaic בזז 'to despoil' in the Targum. Yet such a meaning cannot be said to be clearly attested for the verb, and it is not indicated in this verse either by the ancient versions or by the rabbinic commentators. The Targum and Peshitta suggest 'oppression' (Targum: אנס, which often answers to the Hebrew עָשַׁק; Pesh.: *ṭlm*). The LXX's ἀθετεῖν suggests 'breaking faith'.[1] Amongst the rabbinic commentators, Saadya renders אלגאדר which implies treachery, deceit, and ibn Ezra uses as a synonym the verb למרוד 'to rebel'. Finally, it should be noted that the word בגד occurs elsewhere in Isaiah, in xxiv 16 and xxxiii 1; but these verses are generally and most plausibly regarded as derived from the present text (see below).

The verb שדד is well attested with the meanings 'deal violently with, despoil, devastate' (see B.D.B., K.B. and K.B.[(3)]), and translations of it in this verse, both ancient and modern, show no divergence from this view.

The main problems attaching to the saying are, however, syntactical and exegetical. In the M.T. we are presented with two pairs of qal participles and in each case the first occurrence of the participle is prefixed by the definite article. These defined participles are clearly designed to indicate a specific (enemy?) force. Further, the participles (without article) which in each case follow denote either a present continuous action on which the (enemy?) force is engaged (so the LXX, Vulg. and Pesh.), or an action on which he is about to embark (so Bright in *Peake's Commentary*, p. 504). A third possibility is that suggested by ibn Ezra who gives to each pair of participles respectively a relative and permissive sense: מי שירצה למרוד ולבגוד יוכל 'He who wishes to be rebellious and treacherous will be able to be so.'[2]

The Targum alone of the ancient versions translates the second word in each pair as a passive (e.g. אנוסיא מתאנסין): 'The oppressors are oppressed and the spoilers are despoiled', and this interpretation is followed precisely by Saadya. Rashi and

---

1 See Liddell and Scott, p. 31. The first part of the Vulgate's *qui incredulus est infideliter agit* defies (my) explanation.

2 Galling suggests a variant interpretation of the syntax: for him the defined participles are designations of vocation, the undefined having permissive force: 'Permitted is it for the robber to rob...etc.' The words then form part of the divine commissioning of Elam and Media.

Qimhi, too, seek to understand the phrase in this way, though they attempt to harmonize the M.T. with the interpretation of the Targum; thus Rashi states that השודד is in the accusative, and 'another comes and plunders him [the plunderer]'.[1] For both commentators the reference is to the king of Babylon – once the plunderer, now the plundered.

Such an understanding of the phrase before us may be detected in the Hebrew text of Isa. xxxiii 1 which is generally taken to be a later expansion and reworking of the words of Isa. xxi 2.[2] It is here suggested that the Targum's translation of Isa. xxi 2 is influenced by the M.T. of Isa. xxxiii 1 and that it attempts to harmonize the two.

In attempting to determine who is referred to by the participles of the phrase before us we have noted the view of Rashi and Qimhi that it is the king of Babylon.[3] In the O.T. itself Jeremiah refers to the invading Babylonian foe under the term שׁוֹדֵד (vi 26, xii 12, xv 8), as he does in his oracle against Moab (xlviii 8, 18, 32). On the other hand it may be noted that the word שׁוֹדֵד is used in Isa. xvi 4 of an enemy who attacks Moab, thereby causing fugitives to flee to Jerusalem. The Moab oracles of Isa. xv and xvi are notoriously difficult, but one view is that at least part of them may go back to the time of the Assyrian conquests of Palestine in the latter part of the eighth century. If this is the case it is possible that the verb שדד constitutes a reference to the Assyrian[4] whose coming is elsewhere in Isaiah associated with the words שָׁלָל 'booty', בַּז 'plunder' (viii 3f, x 5f). It should also be noted that in Jewish tradition the word שדד was sometimes associated specifically with Sennacherib; thus Qimhi, notwithstanding his reference to the king of Babylon (see above), states in his comments on Isa. xvi 4, and on xxxiii 1, that the participle שודד is a reference to that Assyrian king.

Finally, it should be noted that amongst modern commentators (e.g.) Dillmann–Kittel, Marti, Procksch and Galling take

---

1 Thereby giving to the second participle an impersonal subject.
2 The same interpretation is also found in the Targum of Isa. xxiv 16.
3 Amongst modern commentators, this view is adopted by e.g. Delitzsch, Ewald, Duhm and Gray.
4 So e.g. Cheyne, *P.I.*; Procksch, and more recently Erlandsson. That Jer. xlviii is clearly dependent on Isa. xvf suggests a pre-exilic date for the latter. See further below.

the view that the words characterize the action or imminent action of the Elamites and Medes and they should be taken closely with the words that follow.

עֲלִי עֵילָם צוּרִי מָדַי. These words constitute perhaps the most important piece of evidence within the text as to its historical background and date. As happens elsewhere (see e.g. vii 2)[1] the feminine singular verbs (here in the imperative) are used in addressing collectively the Elamites and Medes. The verb עלה is used in vii 1 to denote an attack on Jerusalem[2] but it may be taken to mean attack in a general sense rather than ascent.[3]

Apart from the LXX and the Peshitta, the ancient versions and later commentators are unanimous in understanding צורי as an imperative of the well-known verb צור 'to besiege' (B.D.B., p. 848b). The rendering of the Peshitta *wṭwry* 'and the hills of (Media)' clearly indicates that the same Hebrew text was read, though the translators understood the word as the construct plural of the cognate noun צור 'rock' (B.D.B., p. 849b). The resulting sense 'Go up Elam and hills of Media' is hardly satisfactory and it is therefore probable that the Peshitta was mistaken in interpreting the Hebrew word as a noun rather than as a verb.[4]

The LXX's οἱ πρέσβεις (τῶν περσῶν) suggests that it too understood the word as a noun, but here as the construct plural of ציר 'envoy, messenger' (B.D.B., p. 851b). 1QIsᵃ has צירי and this may constitute (manuscript) evidence of the same tradition. Again, however, the LXX's rendering is unlikely to indicate a better way of understanding the text (cf. Seeligmann). No intelligible meaning can be given to their rendering of the preceding words (עלי עילם) ἐπ’ ἐμοὶ οἱ Αἰλαμῖται where עלי is read as the preposition על with first person suffix. It remains more likely that the two words עלי and צורי are verbal forms.

---

1 Cf. G.K. 145k.

2 Cf. Bach, p. 63.

3 Gray's argument – that, because the word is geographically inappropriate to an advance on Babylon, it has been deliberately transferred by the prophet to that use from its proper use in regard to an attack on Jerusalem – is overingenious.

4 It should be noted that Diettrich records the alternative reading *wṭwr*, which he interprets as an imperative of the verb *ṭwr* 'to fly'. If the reading was original, it would not indicate a different Hebrew text. In any case, *wṭwry* (or *wṭwr* in the singular?) 'and hills of' is likely to be the original reading because it can be explained in relation to the M.T.'s צורי, whereas, because no Hebrew word צור is attested with the meaning 'to fly', *wṭwr* meaning 'fly' cannot.

Ibn Ezra compares the verb צוּרִי with Deut. xx 12 where the verb (צַרְתָּ) is used of besieging a city. In this text, however, the verb is followed by an indirect object עָלֶיהָ 'against it' (*sc.* the city). Now, if צוּרִי in Isa. xxi 2 means 'besiege', the problem arises that only here is it used absolutely (i.e. without object). The problem is apparently eased by reference to verse 9 where notice of the fall of Babylon is recorded, and from this point of view the absence of an object is deliberate and heightens the tension of the oracle (cf. Wildberger).

The verb עלה is well attested in the sense 'to go up (toward)' and according to this usage has virtually the sense of English 'to attack' (see B.D.B., p. 748b (2c)). While צוּר 'to besiege' may be regarded as an appropriate parallel expression to עלה 'to attack', the same is also true of the verb צרר 'to show hostility, to vex' (see B.D.B., p. 865b). For this verb too is used of attack and of military harassment (see Num. x 9, xxv 17, xxxiii 55). It is then possible that the consonants צוּרִי constitute an imperative of the verb צרר (צוּרִי > צֹרִי).

Such an understanding of the consonants has the merit that it diminishes the difficulty occasioned by the absolute use of the verb. For while the verb צרר also is not used elsewhere in the bible absolutely (i.e. without object), its meanings may be held to be more capable of such absolute use than are those of the verb צוּר.

Ibn Ezra, commenting on this verse, considers that the whole oracle, from עֲלִי עֵילָם onwards, is put by the prophet into the mouth of the king of Babylon on the grounds that, as is well known, joy rather than terror and despair (verse 3) was the feeling of the prophet as he contemplated the fall of Babylon. He views the phrase before us as a further quotation within the king's speech. Thus the king, when he heard the shouts of the attacking soldiers: 'Go up Elam, etc.', soothed Babylon's sighs by the use of musical instruments. The fact that ibn Ezra has interpreted the oracle in the light of Belshazzar's feast in Dan. v will be considered below, but his view that the phrase before us is a battle-cry of the Elamite and Median soldiers should here be noted.[1] That such quotations are likely to be included in the

---

1 It is possible that Saadya too considered that the phrase was a quotation, for he introduces verse 2 with the phrase 'Its [*sc.* of the terrible land] inhabitants say...'

text of Isaiah may be confirmed by reference to e.g. Isa. vii 2 where the report of an alliance is quoted verbatim.

By contrast, modern commentators are virtually unanimous[1] in seeing the command as on the lips of Yahweh, who thereby commissions the Elamites and Medes to do his will in bringing about the fall of Babylon.[2] For such commentators the Elamites and Medes signify the united Persian kingdom of Cyrus and the attack is that of 539 B.C.[3] To those like Kleinert and Cheyne (*P.I.*) who consider that the prophecy concerns an attack on Babylon at the end of the eighth century, the Elamites and Medes are auxiliary forces in the Assyrian army (as the Elamites are alleged to be in xxii 6), drawn from those parts of Sargon's empire that he had annexed. For further discussion of the historical background, see below.

Verse 2c, כָּל אַנְחָתָה הִשְׁבַּתִּי

The Massoretes (so Vulg. and Pesh.) understand the verb as a hiphil first person singular of the verb שבת. The Vulgate and Peshitta take אנחתה as the noun אנחה 'sighing' with the third feminine singular suffix (*omnem gemitum eius cessare feci*; cf. Pesh.). The LXX witnesses to a different text or to a very different understanding of the text: νῦν στενάξω καὶ παρακαλέσω ἐμαυ-τόν.[4] In the M.T. the final ה of אנחתה is pointed with raphe, though in some MSS. the reading אנחתה is attested.[5] According to Rashi there is no mappiq because the word is emphatic and indicates all the (world-wide) sighing caused by Babylon (cf. Qimhi). Ibn Ezra, however, is content to refer the word אנחתה (with suffix) to Babylon's anxious sighing which is to be stilled by music at the command of her king.

Rashi's interpretation of the pointing of אנחתה on the one hand, and that of ibn Ezra on the other, is reflected in modern

---

1 An exception is Erlandsson, who, like ibn Ezra, sees the phrase as 'the battle cry of the allies in their attacks against Assyria'.

2 For a thorough exposition of this summons to battle as a literary category, see Bach.

3 Cf. Qimhi who states that the whole prophecy concerns the Persians' attack on Babylon.

4 For the view that LXX has probably understood the radicals נח both as a form of אנח (στενάξω) and of נחם (παρακαλέσω), see Goshen-Gottstein.

5 See Goshen-Gottstein (apparatus III).

commentators' views of it. For some the word is understood to be formed with poetic double feminine ending (see e.g. Ewald); for others (so e.g. G.K. 91e, D.K. and Wildberger) the third feminine singular suffix is affixed to the word but it is pronounced softly by reason of the ה which follows it.

On the view that the text means 'I have made all her sighing to cease', a number of exegetical problems present themselves to modern commentators, who differ in their solutions of them. First, it is not clear whose sighings are made to cease; are they those (last sighs) of Babylon (Marti) or of those who sigh over her or of those who have been made to sigh because of her oppression (see e.g. D.K.)? Secondly, who is the subject of השבתי? Thirdly, is that word used appropriately with אנחתה 'sighing' as an object when it is normally used of the ending of e.g. mirth or pride (so Cheyne, *P.I.*, who compares xiii 11 and xvi 10, and Duhm)? The recognition of these difficulties has led many scholars to the conclusion that the text is corrupt and consequently they have sought to emend or to delete it. It is not possible or desirable to list here all such proposals, but the most commonly accepted for אנחתה are those which seek meanings such as 'jubilation' or 'arrogance' (e.g. Duhm גאון, Gray גאותה; cf. Wildberger). More plausible is Eitan's treatment of the word; he obtains for it the meaning 'pride, arrogance' by supposing the word is here cognate to Arabic *nḫwt* which bears this meaning, and by supposing that the initial א is prosthetic. Against his view, however, are the considerations that a Hebrew (א)נחה cognate to Arabic *nḫwt* is not elsewhere attested and neither the versions nor the rabbinic commentators indicate such a tradition.

With regard to השבתי, if that reading is to be retained, the subject can, as Marti maintains, hardly be other than Yahweh; but as he also observes, the sudden introduction of Yahweh as a subject in the first person is harsh.[1] As a consequence many have accepted his initial suggestion[2] that the word be read as a second feminine imperative הַשְׁבִּיתִי parallel to the foregoing imperatives

---

1 Wildberger, on the other hand, argues that the sudden introduction of Yahweh ('I') as the instigator of the events of history is entirely consistent with O.T. views of history.

2 His final conclusion, however, is that the words are a secondary addition which gives expression to Jewish hatred for Babylon and threatens its end as a world power.

(cf. Gray and Procksch). More recently G. R. Driver,[1] following this view of השבתי (though he emends it to the plural form השביתו) has understood the Hebrew אנחתה to be capable of bearing the meaning 'weariness' as well as 'groaning'. This he does by appeal to Accadian *anaḫtu* 'toil, weariness', and he finds such a meaning appropriate to the Hebrew root אנח in Ex. ii 23, Joel i 18 and Lam. i 11. On this view the exhortation to the Elamites and Medes concludes with the words 'Lay aside all weariness' ('No time for weariness!' – N.E.B.).

Driver's solution is certainly a possibility; from the philological point of view it is unexceptionable, and, provided that the text (השבתו) is emended it can be said to fit the context tolerably well. On the other hand there is again no evidence to support it in the ancient versions nor amongst the medieval Jewish commentators and his statement that 'exhaustion' fits the other three texts better than the usual meaning 'sigh' or 'groan' is highly questionable. On balance and unless further evidence becomes available, Driver's view should be treated with caution.

Amongst rabbinic commentators Saadya alone appears not to have taken the usual view of אנחתה. He renders the phrase in which it occurs: גמיע חדרי קד עטלתה, which Derenbourg renders: 'Tous (les cris de): Gare! je les ai supprimés.'[2] It is unfortunately not possible to be certain why Saadya considered the Arabic word *hdr* to be a suitable translation of Hebrew אנחתה, though one possibility is that he saw (or knew a tradition which saw) in אנחתה a form of the root נוח.[3]

If this assumption is correct, appeal may be made to (the late) Isa. xxx 15 and to the noun נחת in the phrase בְּשׁוּבָה וָנַחַת תִּוָּשֵׁעוּן 'in returning and rest shall ye be saved' (R.V.). The words form part of Yahweh's recollection of his appeal to his people to adopt an attitude of quiet, trustful waiting, of its rejection by them in favour of military might, and of Yahweh's subsequent resolution to punish them by force of arms. The oracle (though late) reflects accurately the teachings of Isaiah of Jerusalem (cf. vii 4, 9; viii 6, etc.). In Isa. xxi 2, therefore, the

1 P. 47. He is followed by the N.E.B.
2 Derenbourg's translation does not appear to take into account the first person suffix in חדרי. Does Saadya mean 'I have discontinued all my watchfulness', and intend the phrase to refer to the careless Babylonians?
3 The suggestion was made to me privately and tentatively by S. Morag.

word אנחתה may be a corruption or later adaptation of the word נחת, and the phrase כל(א) נחת(ה) השבתי indicate that, as a result of the disobedience of his people in trusting in military alliances (and such may be the significance of the cry עלי עלם etc.; see below), Yahweh has brought an end to (the possibility of) the quiet, trustful waiting[1] he had previously enjoined.[2]

Verse 3, עַל־כֵּן מָלְאוּ מָתְנַי חַלְחָלָה צִירִים אֲחָזוּנִי כְּצִירֵי יוֹלֵדָה נַעֲוֵיתִי מִשְּׁמֹעַ נִבְהַלְתִּי מֵרְאוֹת׃

The meaning of the words contained in this verse is reasonably clear and their usage to describe terror is well attested (see e.g. Cheyne, *P.I.*; Kaiser). There is some discussion concerning the force of מן in the second part of the verse; thus the LXX, Peshitta and Targum (τὸ μὴ ἀκοῦσαι, *dlᵓ lšmᶜ*, מלשמע) followed by ibn Ezra and Qimhi[3] understand the מן to be privative while the Vulgate (*cum audirem*) understands it to have consequential or causative force (i.e. in consequence of what I hear, I am bent with pain – so e.g. Duhm). There is some force in Marti's argument that על כן at the beginning of the verse conveys adequately the consequential meaning and that, therefore, the מן is best regarded as privative. The verse may be taken to mean: 'in consequence of this (על כן, i.e. in consequence of the revelation of verse 2) pangs have taken hold of me...so that I cannot hear, etc.'

The exegetical problem of this verse (and of verse 4) concerns the identity of the speaker, and it turns on the view taken of the prophecy as a whole. As has been noted above, ibn Ezra poses the problem forcefully:[4] 'I think that the whole of this passage

1 Such a meaning has been suggested for the verb אנוח in Hab. iii 16; for references see B.D.B., p. 628a. That the semantic range of the root נוח extends much further than 'rest, repose' is clear from e.g. O. Eissfeldt's study of the meaning of the word in Isa. vii 2; see *Kleine Schriften*, vol. III (Tübingen, 1966), pp. 124ff. For him נחת in Isa. xxx 15 means specifically 'covenant, fidelity' ('Vertragstreue') and שובה (following Duhm) 'withdrawal from war' ('Abgewandheit vom Kampfe').

2 Obermann suggests that אנחתה concealed נַחְתָּהּ (i.e. נחת with third feminine singular suffix; for him the word denotes 'ease' and he takes the phrase כלא נחתה (כלא for כְּלִי) to mean 'destroy (Babylon's confident) ease'. The difficulty arises, however, that נחת in Isa. xxx 15 is used in a good sense, and נחת 'ease' is better attested in rabbinical Hebrew than in biblical.

3 So e.g. Rosenmüller, D.K., Marti.

4 Friedländer's translation here is not followed precisely, as he has failed to understand ibn Ezra.

from כל אנחתה to the end of the chapter is the speech which the prophet put into the mouth of the king Belshazzar – for it is well known that the prophet rejoiced in the fall of Babylon. How then could he have said "Therefore are my loins filled with pain ..."?[1] So with minor variations Rashi and Qimhi; thus Qimhi states that the prophet speaks in the name of every Babylonian or in the name of Belshazzar. Rashi, however, proposes as an alternative explanation that it is the prophet who laments sympathetically over the punishment of the peoples.

Modern commentators are unanimous in seeing the prophet as the speaker, and have resolved the problem presented by the unexpected horror of a Jewish prophet at the fall of Babylon by following Rashi's second explanation (so e.g. Ehrlich) or by seeing in the words a reflection of the psychological state of the prophet who in ecstasy saw his vision, but did not in that state perceive the salutary implications for his people (see particularly Duhm, and cf. Fohrer).

On a simpler level, Kaiser's observation does much to alleviate the problem. He shows, by reference to xv 5; xvi 9, 11, and Ezek. xxi 11 that the language of personal involvement on the part of a prophet 'may serve simply to emphasize the severity of the events foretold'.[2] But if his observation alleviates the problem, it does not entirely remove it. No other Jewish prophet was struck by horror at the (coming) fall of Babylon in 539 B.C. or regarded that fall as involving anything other than redemption and liberation for his contemporaries.

Verse 4a, תָּעָה לְבָבִי פַּלָּצוּת בִּעֲתָתְנִי

The word לבב may be taken either to refer to the mental faculties of the prophet (so e.g. Saadya, Duhm, Gray, Fohrer) or, as I think, more physically to the heart. For both verses manifestly refer to physical symptoms;[3] further, the word תעה denotes physically 'to wander about' (see B.D.B.) and, predicated of the heart, may be held to describe its fearful commotion; cf. Ps.

1 That the problem was felt also by the Targum can be inferred from the fact that it replaces the first person singular of the M.T. by the third person plural. It is not, however, clear who 'they' are.
2 Cf. Wildberger's similar (though different) observations.
3 Cf. Wildberger's (general) comments, p. 777.

xxxviii 11, and the similar phrase לבי סחרחר lit. 'goes around, is in commotion'.[1]

פלצות בעתתני. There are considerable variations in the versional translations of the phrase, though the general import is clear. LXX: ἡ ἀνομία με βαπτίζει;[2] Vulgate: *tenebrae stupefecerunt me*; Targum: עקא וביעותין אחדונון 'distress and terrors have taken hold of them'; Peshitta: *wṣwrnᵓ ᵓzy ᶜwny* 'dizziness has terrified me'. For פלצות ibn Ezra compares מפלצתה 'her pride' in 1 Kings xv 13 and argues that on this view 'the boasting of the Persians terrified me' (*sc.* King Belshazzar). But he admits the meaning 'trembling' as an alternative, comparing Job ix 6. It is this latter view which is generally accepted by modern lexicographers and commentators.[3] For Qimhi, the phrase indicates 'trembling' and echoes specifically Dan. v 6, וארכבתה דא לדא נקשן 'his (i.e. Belshazzar's) knees smote each other'. The phrase may be rendered 'trembling, convulsions have seized, overwhelmed me'.

Verse 4b, אֶת נֶשֶׁף חִשְׁקִי שָׂם לִי לַחֲרָדָה

From ancient times this phrase has been translated and interpreted in a number of different ways. First, the LXX ἡ ψυχή μου ἐφέστηκεν εἰς φόβον apparently read נפש for נשף and took the phrase as a further definition of (the prophet's?) terror.[4] ἐφέστηκεν construed with ἡ ψυχή as subject may be taken as a way of rendering an impersonal שם לי לחרדה; cf. the Vulgate's *posita est mihi*, the Peshitta's *smw ly* and Saadya's צאר לי 'est devenue pour moi'. This interpretation of the phrase fits the context admirably (cf. Hitzig). The Targum renders by אתר בית רוחצנהון הוה להון לתבר 'their place of refuge has become a destruction (or terror) for them'. נשף is rendered σκότος by Aquila and Theodotion and this denotation is further interpreted to indicate Babylon by Jerome who compares Isa. xiii 2, עַל הַר נִשְׁפֶּה[5] which he renders *in montem caliginosum*. He

---

1 See further my remarks in *V.T.* 23 (1973), 59.
2 On this see Goshen-Gottstein.
3 See e.g. B.D.B., p. 814; מפלצתה, used of an idol in 1 Kings xv 13, is there explained as 'thing to be shuddered at'.
4 The word חשקי is not apparently reproduced in the LXX.
5 See his commentary on Isaiah (Migne, *P.L.*, xxiv, pp. 159, 270). נשפה is not, however, to be connected with נשף but with שפה; see B.D.B., p. 1045. The error probably arises from the phrase הרי נשף in Jer. xiii 16, 'dark mountains' (R.V.).

translates the phrase as a whole: *Babylon dilecta mea posita est mihi in miraculum.*

Ibn Janah shares the view of Aquila and Theodotion and states that נשׁף strictly denotes darkness and twilight (ʾlzlʾm wʾlġbš); he records that some give it here the meaning 'night' as in Job iii 9 and xxiv 15, while others say that it is the twilight of day (i.e. dawn) or of the night (i.e. dusk; for that of dawn he compares Job vii 4). Saadya renders the phrase סחר שעפי 'the dawn of my ardent zeal', which suggests that he was one of the authorities referred to by ibn Janah. That this was also the view of the Peshitta may be inferred from *šwprʾ dṣbyny* lit. 'the beauty of my desire' where *šwprʾ* is probably an internal corruption of *šprʾ* 'dawn'.[1] In his comments on מגן (verse 5) ibn Janah, however, takes the view that the phrase denotes Belshazzar's night of rejoicing (Dan. v). This view is adopted by ibn Ezra ('the night of my pleasure – the night he drank out of the holy vessels'; cf. Dan. v 3), and by Rashi and Qimhi who refer to the first and last verses of Dan. v (Rashi),[2] and to Dan. v 6 (Qimhi). For Rashi an initial defeat of the Persians is the reason for his desiring (חשקי) joy and feasting, though for Qimhi the king was happy because his desire (חשקו) to be made king was accomplished.[3]

Modern commentators are more restrained in their interpretation of the phrase. Almost universally נשׁף is taken to mean 'twilight' and so 'evening'; נשׁף חשקי means 'the twilight that I have longed for' and reference is seen in the phrase either to the evening of rest and recreation expected by the prophet after his harsh experiences of the day[4] or to the evening time when he delighted to have visionary experiences.[5]

An exception to the usual view of the word נשׁף is that advanced by G. R. Driver.[6] For him, the traditional rendering 'the

---

1 So Payne Smith, col. 4274; cf. G. H. Bernstein in *Z.D.M.G.* 3 (1849), 393.
2 The verses describe the feast and the death of the kings as happening on the same night.
3 Such views are quoted by Delitzsch (1) in the name of Umbreit, but they are dismissed out of hand as 'quite impossible'.
4 Marti, Procksch, Fohrer, Wildberger.
5 Kleinert. Others take the view that the harsh vision took place in the evening which the prophet had looked forward to; so e.g. Duhm and Kaiser; the latter freely admits that it is not certain.
6 See *Von Ugarit nach Qumran* (Eissfeldt Festschrift; *Z.A.W.* Bei. 77), ed. J. Hempel and L. Rost (Berlin, 1958).

twilight of my desire etc.' is 'a strange mixture of phrases', and consequently he seeks to find a somewhat different meaning for the word נשף by appeal to the Arabic cognate *nsf*. Because the verb *nasufa* can mean (vIIIth theme) 'whispered (words)' and the noun *nasîf* 'truce, secret conversation' he posits for the noun נשף the meaning 'faintest suspicion, trace' and for the phrase נשף חשקי the meaning 'my faintest (i.e. scarcely breathed) wish', rendering the sentence as a whole 'my faintest wish has been turned into anxiety for me'. Driver continues by appealing to Saadya's use of the word '*siḥru* "anything, of which the chance of obtaining it is slight and slender"'' which, says Driver, 'brings out the sense of the Hebrew word quite well'.

Two criticisms may be directed against Driver's theory. First, his rendering 'faintest (i.e. scarcely breathed) wish' is speculative in that he gives to נשף a particular meaning akin to that which he claims for לחש in Isa. xxvi 16 (i.e. lit. 'whisper') 'a very small amount'. Now this is not certainly the denotation of לחש in that verse (for another view, see B.D.B.) nor is it clearly attested for the Arabic root *nsf* to which Driver appeals.

Secondly, his appeal to Saadya's rendering is ill-founded. The word סחר is clearly Arabic *sḥr* 'dawn'[1] which answers to the well-attested Hebrew word נשף 'twilight' (see on ibn Janah above).

To return for a moment to Saadya's view that נשף denotes 'dawn', it is possible, perhaps, to see in the phrase a reference to the morning of salvation which is probably alluded to in the Dumah oracle of Isa. xxi 11f (cf. Ps. xlvi 6) and in Isa. xvii 14. On this view the dawn of peace that the prophet had hoped for is, in consequence of the dire contents of his vision, changed to an occasion for horror and trembling. Thus Saadya understands the whole phrase as the cause or occasion of the prophet's alarm (אד סחר שעפי צאר לי אזעאגא 'puisque l'aurore de mon amour est devenue pour moi une épouvante').

Verse 5, עָרֹךְ הַשֻּׁלְחָן צָפֹה הַצָּפִית אָכוֹל
שָׁתֹה קוּמוּ הַשָּׂרִים מִשְׁחוּ מָגֵן:

The verse as a whole is generally taken to depict a third detailed scene of the prophet's vision because what is set forth clearly

---

1 And so it is translated by Derenbourg.

differs from that of the opening scene (verses 1 ff) and from that which follows (verses 6 ff).

The infinitive absolutes which characterize the first half of the verse are either taken as imperatives[1] or as denoting description in a lively narration.[2]

ערך השלחן. At first sight no problems are presented by the phrase, for the meaning 'prepare, set in order the tables' (i.e. the dishes upon it – so B.D.B.) is clearly attested elsewhere (see e.g. Prov. ix 2; Ezek. xxiii 41; Pss. xxiii 5, lxxviii 19) and in this way the phrase is almost universally translated. Reference is consequently seen in the words to the feasting Babylonians soon to be roused from their revels by the writing on the wall or by the death of Belshazzar (cf. the rabbinic comments on verse 4). Some scholars[3] take the phrase to indicate the nocturnal feasting in the centre of Babylon mentioned by Herodotus and by Xenophon as having taken place on the eve of its fall to Cyrus (for references etc., see below).

צפה הצפית. Considerable difficulties attach to these words (the second of which is a hapax legomenon) and the problem of their interpretation turns largely on their being understood closely with the preceding phrase. The ancient versions[4] clearly connect both words with the root צפה 'to look out or about' which also occurs in verse 6. The reference is then to the setting up of a watch simultaneously with preparing for a meal (so e.g. Saadya and Qimhi; the latter states that some Babylonians, fearful of the Persians, urged that a watch be set).

On the other hand, reference at this point to a watch may be said to be inconsistent with the ease and relaxation which mark the beginning of the feast; it is likely that this consideration lies behind the variety of alternative explanations advanced by the rabbinic commentators. For ibn Janah צפה הצפית means *sfff ʾlṣfwf* 'arrange, set in order the rows'[5] and *ʾlṣfwf* is either

---

1 G.K. 113bb; so the ancient versions and e.g. Rashi, ibn Ezra, Procksch.
2 G.K. 113ff; so e.g. Saadya, D.K., Marti, Kaiser, Fohrer, Wildberger.
3 So e.g. Rosenmüller and Delitzsch; others (e.g. Cheyne, *P.I.*; Marti, and Kaiser) are cautious about the identification.
4 The LXX excepted; the phrase is not apparently rendered there. Whether or not it was in the text before the translator is not certainly known. Ziegler (*Untersuchungen*) takes the view that it was omitted in the LXX because the translator did not understand it.
5 Ibn Janah clearly uses the verb *ṣf* because of its similarity in form to Hebrew צפה. But he lists the latter word under צ"פ"ה and not under צ"פ"ף.

rows of the food on the table or the ranks of the diners at the table.[1]

Ibn Janah goes on to state that the verb צפה is similar in meaning to ערך 'to set in order' and he compares the juxta-position of the two words in this verse with that in Ps. v 5.

Ibn Ezra notes that the word צפית occurs only here and says that, in his opinion, the phrase means 'make melody' (נגון) but he gives no indication how he achieves this meaning. For Rashi and Qimhi (as one suggestion) צפית refers again to an aspect of Belshazzar's feast, viz. to lighting the lights; and for this Qimhi refers to Genesis R. 63 (on Gen. xxxv 34) which, referring to Isa. xxi 5, states, in the name of R. Abba bar Kahana, 'there are places where they call a lamp צפיתא'.

Modern commentators who do not accept the meaning 'set the watch' usually accept Hitzig's theory that the phrase means the spreading of rugs or mats upon which diners reclined.[2] Cheyne (*I.B.I.*) takes a similar view and compares Jewish Aramaic צִיפְתָּא[3] 'matting, mat'. With this explanation, as Delitzsch observes, there is the difficulty that it is without support in biblical usage and is not attested by any old tradition.

אכול שתה. The meaning of these words is clear, though Duhm (so also e.g. Marti) raises the important question whether they should be deleted as a superfluous later addition. There is no manuscript or versional evidence to support this view, though it may be noted that the words occur in the following chapter of Isaiah (xxii 13), and it is possible that they found their way thence to this chapter as an interpretative gloss on the difficult phrase צפה הצפית.

קומו השרים משחו מגן. The phrase as a whole is usually taken to indicate the sudden call to arms directed at the feasting nobles.

מגן is understood to denote specifically 'shield(s)' by the ancient versions other than the Targum, which renders the word more generally by זינא 'weapons'. משחו indicates the preparation (LXX: ἑτοιμάσατε) or taking up of (Vulg.: *arripite*)[4] the shield, though the Targum furnishes a more

---

1 Eitan accepts ibn Janah's explanation of the phrase.
2 Hitzig's argument that the root צפה here is a form of צפח and may be compared to Arabic *sfḥ* is most unlikely.
3 For this word, see Jastrow, p. 1279.
4 For Dathius' view that the Vulgate read משכו (with כ), see Rosenmüller.

general meaning with מריקו וצחצחו 'polish and make bright (your weapons)'.[1] Rashi considers that משחו denotes oiling the shield and for this practice he compares 2 Sam. i 21.

Modern commentators generally follow such interpretations though different views are held of the reason for oiling shields. For some (e.g. Delitzsch; cf. Kaiser) the purpose was to make the surface slippery and thereby to facilitate the deflection from it of missiles and blows. Others (e.g. Duhm, Gray) suppose that the straps of the shields are oiled so that they should not cut into the arms of the soldiers.[2]

A very different view of the phrase is taken by other rabbinic commentators. Saadya understands the verse to depict a people who feast while their leaders arise and anoint a king from their number (וקד קאם רויסאהם ומסחו אלמלך מנהם). It is not possible to be certain what Saadya in general thought the words depicted, but it is likely that his views are reflected by ibn Ezra. He, accepting the view that מגן means king, comments that Darius was anointed king in the same night that Belshazzar was killed.[3] Apart from the question whether the phrase has to do with Belshazzar's death and its consequence, Saadya's view of the meaning of משחו מגן is possible and deserves consideration.[4]

Ibn Janah presents us with yet a third view of משחו מגן, though for him too the phrase indicates the circumstances after Belshazzar's death. When the pleasant evening (נשף חשקי) becomes terror (לחדרה) after the death of the king, the tables are left by the diners who wipe them down. מגן, then, for ibn Janah denotes 'tables'[5] and משחו means ʾmsḥwʾ (wipe off) or

1 Qimhi quotes the Targum with approval.

2 Fohrer's view (cf. also Wildberger) that the shields are consecrated by anointing for use in a holy war is fanciful. There is no clear evidence to support his assertion.

3 Similarly ben Bilam and Qimhi. The former thinks that the words קומו···מגן are a quotation of the princes' resolution to appoint a successor to Belshazzar.

4 Ibn Ezra and ben Bilam think that the word can denote 'king' because a king protects his people like a shield. For discussion of מגן in a number of texts having the meaning 'ruler', see J. D. Michaelis, *Neue Orientalische und Exegetische Bibliothek*, vol. VII (1790), pp. 178ff, and 205; G. R. Driver in *J.T.S.* 33 (1932), 44, and 34 (1933), 383f; M. Dahood, *The Psalms* (Anchor Bible, 3 vols., Garden City, N.Y., 1966–70), indices; J. Barr in *Bibliotheca Ephemeridum Lovaniensium* 33 (1974), 45ff.

5 He gives no explanation of this view of מגן other than using the synonym שלחן and the translation *mʾydt*.

ʾnzʿwʾ (strip bare). In general the reference is to the removal of food from the table, though משח specifically denotes here the polishing movement of the hand upon the table.[1]

Ibn Janah's view may rest upon his giving to משח a meaning attested rather for Arabic msḥ than for Hebrew משח. No other instance of the verb with the denotation 'wipe down' or 'clear away (food)' is attested in the O.T. A further difficulty is that ibn Janah gives no etymological grounds for his view that מגן here means 'table'.[2]

It was observed above that the interpretation of צפה הצפית is often influenced by its juxtaposition to ערך השלחן. If the latter phrase means 'prepare the tables' then it is likely that צפה הצפית denotes some aspect of the feast. The argument is, however, entirely reversed by one modern scholar, K. Galling. He takes the view that צפה הצפית means 'keep watch' and, as in verse 6, the words are to be derived from the root צפה (see above). ערך השלחן is a corruption of an original עָרֹךְ הַשֶּׁלַח[3] 'men prepare their weapons, and keep watch...' These preparations are the Persians' response to Yahweh's call to take up arms against Babylon (verse 2b), the signal itself being given by the words קומו השרים which follow; אכל ושתה are understood as a later explanatory gloss defining the significance of 'the table'.

Galling's view of the historical background of the oracle is discussed elsewhere. However, it may be suggested that his emendation, which involves the alteration of only one letter of the consonantal text, and the deletion of two words (the authenticity of which may be doubted on other grounds; see above) is worth consideration. For, first, it enables us to retain the best-attested meanings for the words צפה and הצפית and, secondly, it avoids the necessity of making a number of suppositions as to the sequence of events (e.g. feasting followed by call to arms). It may be added that ערך is clearly attested elsewhere of preparing weapons for battle (Jer. xlvi 3, מגן וצנה; 1 Chron. xii 9, צנה ורמח).

---

1 ʾǧry ʾlyd ʿlyh – the same movement that is employed in the anointing of persons.

2 Cf. ben Bilam's similar criticisms of ibn Janah.

3 השלחן > השלח ו···.

Verse 6, כִּי כֹה אָמַר אֵלַי אֲדֹנָי לֵךְ הַעֲמֵד
הַמְצַפֶּה אֲשֶׁר יִרְאֶה יַגִּיד:

The verse seems to depict a third and different scene. No difficulties are presented with regard to the meaning of the words,
though differing views are set forth concerning their exegesis.

אֵלַי is usually taken to indicate the prophet himself. For.
Qimhi the prophet is, as it were, in Babylon, and Yahweh
speaks to him as a representative of the princes of Babylon,
who, concerned about the advance of the Medes and Persians,
set a watch.[1] That Qimhi reflects Saadya's view is probable; the
latter translates אֵלַי by עֵנָّא 'concerning us' and העמד by אוקפו
לכם 'set for yourselves (a watchman)'. The pronouns in Saadya's
translation are defined by his interpretation of the beginning
of verse 5 ('It is a people whose tables are prepared etc.').

מצפה suggests 'watchman, lookout' to all the ancient versions
and to the rabbinic commentators. For Rashi the reference is
specifically to the prophet Habakkuk and he compares Hab. ii
1 עַל מִשְׁמַרְתִּי אֶעֱמֹדָה 'I will stand upon my watch' (R.V.). Thus,
Isaiah is promised by God that Habakkuk will prophesy in the
future the fall of Babylon. For Rashi the identification is made
certain by the reference in verse 8 to אריה which, by *gîmatriyâ*
(i.e. the numerical value of the letters), is equivalent to Habakkuk. While it is impossible to accept this far-fetched and strained
exegesis of מצפה, Rashi's comparison with Hab. ii 1 (which also
contains the verb אצפה) is valuable as indicating that another
prophet uses the imagery of the watchman and of looking out.[2]
On the basis of such comparative evidence modern scholars
(following Ewald, Duhm[3] and Marti) have seen in the watchman a reference rather to the prophet's *alter ego* which is the
subject of visionary experiences than to an actual separate
personality appointed to make the observations which the
prophet then interprets. It is possible that ibn Ezra held a
similar view (though of course without a specifically psychological account), for he notes that the prophet did not appoint

1 Obermann adopts this view enthusiastically.
2 But cf. Wildberger's (implied) caution against too-facile attempts to harmonize
  Isa. xxi with Habakkuk, whether it is done by textual emendation or by resort
  to psychological theories.
3 His account from the psychological point of view is particularly impressive.

a watchman in reality but only בדרך נבואה 'in his vision'.[1] Buhl and B. Stade[2] find this sort of explanation quite unacceptable as being 'unnatural and quite without analogy' (Buhl). Consequently, Buhl, referring to the LXX's reading ὃ ἂν ἴδῃς (i.e. second masculine singular) for the M.T.'s יראה (third masculine singular), proposes the emendation: לְכוּ עֲמֹדָה מְצַפֶּה אֲשֶׁר תִּרְאֶה הַגֵּד 'Come take your stand, O watchman; relate what you see.'[3] Such alteration of the text, however, is unjustified. The LXX's rendering is likely to be merely interpretative and does not suggest a different text (cf. Goshen-Gottstein). Further, that the prophet should speak figuratively[4] of his function is, as has been shown, quite reasonable and, in view of the evidence of Hab. ii 1 (cf. also Isa. xxi 11), likely.[5]

The remaining problem of the verse concerns the precise force of the opening כי. For the majority (e.g. D.K., Duhm) the particle denotes the introduction to the details of the harsh vision of verse 2, i.e. the news of Babylon's fall. For others (e.g. Marti) it introduces the reason for the prophet's terror. Galling, who emends the text of the previous verse (see above), considers that the particle affords a connexion between verses 5 and 6 which both concern the opening of the war by the Persians. The force given to כי, however, depends entirely upon the view taken of the shape of the prophecy as a whole and it is not possible here to resolve the question finally.[6]

Verse 7, וְרָאָה רֶכֶב צֶמֶד פָּרָשִׁים רֶכֶב חֲמוֹר
רֶכֶב גָּמָל וְהִקְשִׁיב קֶשֶׁב רַב־קָשֶׁב:

If waw consecutive is prefixed to third person singular masculine verbs, then the first half of the verse may be a subordinate

---

1 Cf. Wildberger (who follows J. Hanel); he repudiates the *alter ego* theory, preferring to think of the prophet as appointing an imaginary watchman in his trances and visions.

2 See *Z.A.W.* 8 (1888), 157ff, 165ff.

3 Stade suggests the modification לְכָה עֲמֹד הַמִּצְפֶּה 'Go, set yourself on the watch', etc.

4 At least figuratively; I do not regard myself as competent to judge whether a psychological account is justified on the evidence. Cf. Kaiser's comments Band those of Wildberger.

5 Another objection to the proposal to emend is that mentioned by Wildberger; emendation of this verse requires consequential emendation of verse 8.

6 Cf. Wildberger's observations. For him the usual 'for' is out of place as there is no logical connexion between the verse and what precedes it, and to claim here an asseverative force for it is mere expediency.

temporal clause. Thus, ibn Ezra renders אם ראה...יקשיב 'When he sees...then shall he pay attention.'[1] On this view the phrase constitutes a continuation of the divine command of verse 6. Saadya, by contrast, takes the perfects to be prefixed by simple waw and consequently translates the verse as an account of the (Babylonians') fulfilment of the order[2] (...פאוקפנאה וראי 'So we set (the watchman) in his place and he saw...').

The LXX's καὶ εἶδον (i.e. first person) may be regarded as an accommodation to its (free) translation of the previous verse rather than as implying that it read וְרָאִיתִ. Buhl, however, takes the view that an original וראיתָ was read וראית by the LXX. He repoints והקשיב as an imperative and takes the verse to mean 'When you see...then pay attention.' The interpretation differs little in substance from that of ibn Ezra (see above) and, as the latter is entirely appropriate, Buhl's emendations may be judged superfluous.

Considerable uncertainty attaches to the precise meaning of the terms used of what is to be (or was) seen. In particular the words רכב and פרש have been variously understood.

(1) רכב (first occurrence); the LXX renders ἀναβάτας 'riders' while Symmachus and Jerome render 'chariot' (ἅρμα *currum*). Targum's רתך is capable of either meaning[3] as is the Peshitta's *rkwbʾ*.[4] Saadya renders כיולא 'horses' but ibn Barun compares for this verse Arabic *rkb*[5] 'a party of riders above ten (on camels)'. Ibn Barun's view is adopted by a number of modern commentators (e.g. D.K., Marti, Gray, Kissane), while others insist that the word is better attested in the bible with the meaning 'chariot(ry)' (e.g. Stade, Procksch, Galling, S. Mowinckel, Fohrer, Wildberger). Ibn Janah appears to agree with this view and states that רכב can properly denote chariotry collectively and he illustrates this view by quoting 2 Kings vii 14, ויקחו שני רכב סוסים 'they took therefore two chariots with horses' (so R.V.), and this verse.

(2) פרש. Symmachus (ἵππων) and Jerome (*equitum*) take the

---

1 See G.K. 164b (4); so e.g. Marti, Procksch.
2 Similarly, Stade thinks the verse relates what the prophet saw and is not part of the command; so also Delitzsch.
3 Cf. Stenning: 'cavalcade (*or* chariot)'.
4 Cf. Brockelmann and Payne Smith.
5 Wechter, p. 119. For *rkb* meaning riders, horses, cavalcade, caravan, troop, etc., see e.g. Wehr.

word to denote horses and the three words רכב צמד פרשים together to indicate two-horse chariot(s).[1] The LXX, Targum and the Peshitta on the other hand take פרשים to mean pairs of 'riders' (ἱππεῖς; פרשין; pršyn);[2] the Targum further indicates for the pair of 'riders' that one rode upon an ass, the other upon a camel.[3] 1QIs[a] may indicate the same tradition, for the reading רוכב is there found for the second[4] and third occurrences of the word רכב in the verse. Rashi appears to follow the Targum and he suggests that the two riders on their respective mounts constitute a symbol of the Medes and Persians.[5]

Saadya renders פרשים by אלפרסאן 'horsemen' and takes צמד פרשים to denote ואזואגא מן אלפרסאן 'some pairs of horsemen' amongst other riders who were mounted on asses and camels.[6] This view is adopted by a number of modern scholars who see in the phrase 'couples of horsemen' i.e. horsemen riding in a column in pairs (e.g. Hitzig, D.K., Marti, Gray).[7]

This second interpretation of פרשים has been vigorously challenged by Galling (Z.Th.K. 53 (1956), 129ff) and Mowinckel (V.T. 12 (1962), 278ff) whose conclusions are virtually identical. Galling argues from the evidence of usage that סוס ורכב used together denotes horses and war chariots and that פרשים[8] are specifically war horses yoked to chariots. He states that there was no comprehensive term to denote chariot riders, who, in any case, comprised archers etc. In Isa. xxi 9 the unique expression רכב איש must be explained by reference to the contrast it affords to רכב חמר.[9] רכב חמר indicates the two-

---

1 So e.g. Galling, Mowinckel and Wildberger; for their exposition of the words רכב and פרש, see below. Stade's view that a (dispatch) rider is mounted on a pair of chariot horses, unhitched for the purpose of speedily bringing the news of Babylon's fall, is absurd. As Duhm observes, one horse would be unhitched in such circumstances.
2 In Aramaic and Syriac the word does not carry the meaning 'horse'.
3 So perhaps the Peshitta: rkwbᵓ dtryn pršyn drkyb ḥmrᵓ wdrkyb gmlᵓ.
4 The waw is here added secundus manus; so Goshen-Gottstein. The reading was earlier proposed conjecturally by Buhl and Stade.
5 So amongst moderns Procksch, who sees in them representatives of Elam and Media.
6 Does רכאב indicate that he read רכב (second occurrence) as רֹכֵב?
7 Hitzig and Marti observe that even if פרשים here denotes 'horses' then the riders are included in that definition; but their observation depends on their taking רכב (first occurrence) not as chariots but as a cavalcade.
8 פרשים is likely to be a North Syrian–Aramaic technical term (? denoting a particular breed of horse) adopted by Hebrew.
9 So, mutatis mutandis, רכב גמל.

wheeled baggage wagon pulled by asses, by the side of which the driver walked. The terms רכב (verse 7) and רכב איש (verse 9) are both further defined by the term צמד פרשים which means (chariot with a) 'pair of war horses'. The phrase רכב צמד פרשים means two-horse chariots, and for this 2 Kings ix 25 is quoted as evidence.

רכב איש in verse 9 denotes manned chariots as opposed to wagons. Thus, as Galling understands the terms, the beasts indicate the nature of the vehicle which they pull (cf. English 'horse-carriage', 'motor-carriage'). Galling's account of these terms, while it is soundly based on the evidence of usage in the O.T., is not wholly convincing in regard to two phrases in Isa. xxi. First, רכב איש (verse 9) as a manned chariot; by analogy with his account of רכב חמור etc., רכב איש ought strictly to mean a cart pulled by men and not a manned chariot. Secondly, it is doubtful whether the word רכב was ever used to denote baggage wagons as opposed to chariots, and certainly, as Wildberger observes (p. 782), there is no evidence in the O.T. that asses or camels pulled such wagons. That they should have pulled chariots is *a fortiori* most unlikely.

According to Galling, the correct denotation for פרשים was obscured because cavalry, and horses bred specifically for the purpose, later became the norm in the Orient. When the two-wheel war chariot, still prevalent in the seventh century B.C., began to fade into the background, eventually to vanish, the distinction between *paraš* (= chariot horse) and *parraš* (with geminated resh[1]), to which the Massoretic פָּרָשִׁים bears witness, was coined (*parraš* with the meaning 'trooper').

The secondary meaning, 'cavalry', probably belongs to the time of cavalry par excellence, i.e. to the time of the Persians.

If, as seems probable, Galling's views[2] are substantially correct the use of the terms in this verse may be important as evidence for the dating of the prophecy.

---

1 On this further Gesenius–Buhl. Galling compares the form רִכָּב.

2 Mowinckel's views are virtually identical. His treatment of Isa. xxi 7 and 9, however, lacks precision; thus e.g. he adopts L. Koehler's 'train' for רכב and thereby seems to imply that the asses and camels themselves bore the baggage, all of which contradicts his thesis that רכב means 'chariotry'; further, he quite fails to give an adequate account of רכב איש. For these reasons I have preferred to follow Galling's account. For an older argument to the effect that פרשים means 'horses' and never 'riders', see W. R. Arnold in *J.B.L.* 24 (1905), 45ff. For further discussion of the etymology of the word פרש, see D. R. Ap-Thomas.

וְהִקְשִׁיב קֶשֶׁב רַב־קָשֶׁב. For the emphatic expression 'he shall pay very great attention', cf. with Marti Isa. xxviii 21 and lxiii 7.

Verse 8, וַיִּקְרָא אַרְיֵה עַל־מִצְפֶּה אֲדֹנָי אָנֹכִי עֹמֵד
תָּמִיד יוֹמָם וְעַל־מִשְׁמַרְתִּי אָנֹכִי נִצָּב כָּל־הַלֵּילוֹת:

ויקרא אריה. The Vulgate, Aquila, Symmachus, Theodotion and the Targum appear to confirm the M.T.'s אריה 'lion'. The lion is taken to be the subject of the verb by Saadya and Rashi, the latter explaining that by *gîmatriyâ* the prophet Habakkuk is meant.[1]

Theodotion's Ἀριήλ may indicate a tradition that the word is to be explained by reference to Isa. xv 9 where the remnant of the Moabites are destined for the lion. Here the LXX renders אריה by Ἀριήλ (cf. LXX, Isa. xxix 1). On this latter verse ibn Ezra states that אריה is a reference to the king of Assyria.[2] In a somewhat similar way, Qimhi takes the view that אריה in Isa. xxi 8 contains a reference to the Medes and Persians.

Ibn Ezra and ben Bilam interpret אריה as if a kaph were prefixed to it and for the construction they compare (respectively) Deut. iv 24 and Prov. xi 22, 'And he cried like a lion.' This view of the phrase is adopted by a number of modern scholars,[3] amongst them Rosenmüller who compares Rev. x 3.

1QIs[a] records the variant reading הראה 'the seer' for אריה and this is widely adopted as the most likely solution as it furnishes a subject for the verb ויקרא.[4] It is interesting to record that it was proposed as an emendation before the discovery of 1QIs[a] by R. Lowth in 1778, and adopted as such by Procksch.[5]

The remainder of the words of this verse are tolerably clear, and the divergences in the versions etc. are minor. It is worth noting, however, that the Peshitta interprets the speaker as God who addresses (presumably) the prophet and informs him that he (God) is continually standing upon his watchtower day and night.

1 Cf. Ibn Ezra, who records the tradition as from the Midrash.
2 Cf. Qimhi, notwithstanding the fact that he and Rashi think primarily of Nebuchadnezzar.
3 E.g. Delitzsch, D.K.
4 So e.g. *B.H.S.* and N.E.B., Fohrer, Wildberger. The verb ראה occurs in verses 6f.
5 Though he attributes it to Sievers. Wildberger wrongly mentions Lohmann as the originator of the suggestion.

The most natural interpretation, however, is that which
assumes that the prophet (or his *alter ego*) is speaking and that
he is expressing his impatient suspense as he waits for fulfilment
of the promised vision. Marti argues that the words between
ויקרא אראה (thus he emends) and הנה (verse 9) are an interpola-
tion inspired by Isa. lxii 6 where the watchmen continually
look out for the dawn at the end of the time of judgement. He
regards the words as impairing the structure and parallelism of
this part of the oracle and as contradicting the meaning of verse
4 which implies that the prophet received his dreadful vision in
the same evening in which he received his order (verse 7).

On the other hand, it is possible to argue that Isa. lxii 6 is
dependent upon this prophecy for some of its phrases and it is
likely that the words here convey the protestation of the prophet
(or his watchman) that he has faithfully obeyed the command
to pay very great attention.

A number of the words and expressions of the verse are found
in Hab. ii 1, as has been noted above. For discussion of this, see
below, pp. 123ff.

Verse 9a, וְהִנֵּה־זֶה בָא רֶכֶב אִישׁ צֶמֶד פָּרָשִׁים
וַיַּעַן וַיֹּאמֶר נָפְלָה נָפְלָה בָּבֶל׃

The verse may be regarded as the climax of the prophecy and
the words 'fallen is Babylon' as the burden of its contents.

רכב איש is taken to refer to a single rider by the LXX, Vulgate
and Peshitta. For the Targum there comes a cavalcade of men
(רתך אנש) and with them a pair of horsemen (ועמיה זוג פרשין).
This interpretation is adopted by ibn Ezra who states that עם is
to be supplied before צמד פרשים, though he says nothing of the
sort in regard to verse 7.

Saadya, like the LXX etc., thinks that the phrase denotes
the advent of a lone horseman behind whom are a pair of
riders. The former addresses the prophet with the words
'Babylon is fallen.' For Qimhi, on the other hand, the phrase
denotes the arrival of the Persian army in Babylon.

The LXX's ἀναβάτης συνωρίδος suggests to Procksch that it
translated רכב צמד פרשים (as in verse 7) and that איש was not
present in the text that it translated. He concludes that (רכב)
איש is an explanatory gloss which attempts to define פרשים as

'men' rather than 'horses'. Procksch's view is attractive on the grounds that the word איש does not qualify רכב in verse 7 and because no satisfactory account of the meaning of רכב איש has been given. It should be noted that the phrase (ב)רכב אדם פרשים occurs in xxii 6. It is possible that the text of xxii 6, if indeed it is authentic,[1] has influenced the text of the verse before us just as xxi 5 may have been influenced by xxii 13 (see on verse 5 above).

For the first part of the verse modern commentators direct themselves to the question why the vision, by comparison with verse 7, contains an apparently abbreviated description of what comes. For some, what the prophet sees in verse 9 is not the same as what is described in verse 7. For example, Delitzsch thinks of a smaller cavalcade whose function is to carry the news of Babylon's fall, whereas verse 7 refers to the whole Persian army approaching Babylon. Other commentators, however (e.g. D.K.), think that the reference in both verses is the same and that the abbreviation of the account of a previously described and expected vision is entirely natural (cf. Wildberger).

On the view that verse 7 contains a sentence with protasis and apodosis (see above), the use in verse 9 of the demonstrative זה may indicate what in the event the prophet in his vision actually saw, i.e. רכב צמד פרשים as opposed to רכב חמור etc. On this supposition, it is further possible that verse 7 lists a number of alternative objects of sight for which the prophet is to wait, i.e. either רכב צמד פרשים or רכב חמור or רכב גמל. On the other hand זה is probably used here merely as an enclitic (cf. B.D.B., p. 261 4g), and in this case it has no demonstrative force.

ויען ויאמר. The subject of the verbs is not expressed (so the ancient versions). For ibn Ezra it is all the persons of the cavalcade mentioned in the earlier part of the verse, and *mutatis mutandis* for Saadya it is the lone horseman.[2] Qimhi, on the other hand, regards the watchman (i.e. the prophet) as the subject of the verb (so e.g. D.K., Duhm, Marti), and Kaiser, comparing e.g. Amos vii 8, Jer. i 12, Zech. i 14f,[3] thinks that

---

1 Marti, following Grätz, believes that the phrase רכב צמד (*sic*) פרשים in xxii 6 is a gloss derived from xxi 7.
2 So, amongst moderns, e.g. Delitzsch, Buhl, Stade, Procksch.
3 For the full list, see his commentary.

God is the subject. Wildberger, too, argues that Yahweh (or, as in Zech. iv 1ff, his angel) is the subject of the verbs; he reveals to the prophet the meaning of the vision (cf. Zech. ii 4). For Wildberger the use of first person suffixes (מדשתי/בן־גרני) in the following verse tells in favour of this explanation. On balance, however, it seems most natural to see the watchman as the subject of the verbs.[1]

נפלה בבל. The repetition of the all-important cry is, as Qimhi observes, emphatic. The Targum interprets the repetition: 'Babylon has fallen and is also about to fall (נפלת ואף עתידא למיפל)', and this interpretation is further explained by Rashi who states that the first fall is that at the hands of the Persians and that the second is at God's hand and to this Isa. xiii 19 alludes ('And Babylon…shall be as when God overthrew Sodom and Gomorrah' – R.V.). While this interpretation is clearly contrived and fanciful, it represents two possible interpretations of the verb נפלה; it is either an historic perfect (with the messenger(s) as the speaker) or a prophetic perfect (with God or the prophet as the speaker).[2]

Verse 9b, וְכָל־פְּסִילֵי אֱלֹהֶיהָ שִׁבַּר לָאָרֶץ:

The verb שבר is best regarded as having an impersonal third masculine singular subject, for which the Vulgate, Targum and Peshitta (so Saadya) make use of the passive voice. Some modern commentators, however, take God as the subject of שבר (so e.g. Rosenmüller, Delitzsch and Procksch; the last, however, prefers to emend to שֻׁבְּרוּ on the evidence of the LXX).[3]

Amongst the versions, the LXX alone appears to diverge widely from the M.T.: καὶ πάντα τὰ ἀγάλματα αὐτῆς καὶ τὰ χειροποίητα αὐτῆς for כל פסילי אלהיה. The rendering may be a doublet of an earlier text which read פְּסִילֶיהָ (i.e. of Babylon) or אֱלֹהֶיהָ only (cf. Gray).

---

1 Wildberger's argument that it would be strange if ויקרא in verse 8 were expanded by ויען ויאמר in this verse is not convincing. The verb ענה is used not only to denote 'answering, replying', but also 'speaking in view of circumstances' and 'testifying'; see B.D.B.

2 The LXX does not repeat the verb and on this evidence Procksch proposes to delete the second נפלה. Such emendation is hardly justified; cf. Wildberger.

3 M. Dahood's suggestion (in *Biblica* 40 (1959), 165) that ארץ here denotes the underworld may be rejected; he adduces no arguments in its favour other than to say that it is 'probable'. Dahood follows Cross and Freedman (in *J.N.E.S.* 14 (1955), 247ff), but they say even less than Dahood in support of the theory.

For the rest, the closing phrase of the verse is of interest as possible evidence for the dating of the prophecy. For, as is widely observed among modern commentators, Cyrus did not shatter idols, but, on the contrary, was sympathetic to the gods of the peoples whom he vanquished. Further, Babylon fell into his hands without fighting. Those who take the view that the oracle concerns the fall of Babylon in 539 B.C. emphasize that we have here no *vaticinium ex eventu* and that, in that he foretold what did not happen, the prophet was mistaken or merely represented a motif which belongs to the prophetic *Gattung* – the fall of a world power (so e.g. D.K., Duhm, Gray and Wildberger). For other scholars, who on various grounds regard the prophecy as indicating a fall of Babylon in Assyrian times, such considerations constitute further evidence pointing to that conclusion (so e.g. Cheyne, *P.I.*, p. 126, and Erlandsson, p. 91).

Verse 10, מְדֻשָׁתִי וּבֶן־גָּרְנִי אֲשֶׁר שָׁמַעְתִּי מֵאֵת יְהוָֹה
צְבָאוֹת אֱלֹהֵי־יִשְׂרָאֵל הִגַּדְתִּי לָכֶם:

The verse appears to contain a reflection of the prophet on the import of his message, and the first person suffix attached to מדשתי 'my threshed one' and בן גרני refers to the prophet or to God (so Qimhi) in whose name the prophet speaks. Ibn Ezra mentions both interpretations as possibilities, adding a third: that it refers to the רכב איש.[1]

For Saadya מדשתי and בן גרני are references to Babylon which is so described in its overthrow (פצארת כמדאסי 'She [Babylon] has become like threshed corn etc.'). Similarly, ibn Ezra and Qimhi regard Babylon as the object of the threshing, though the former mentions as a possibility that בן גרני contains a reference to Israel as the pure corn kept in the threshing floor.

The LXX clearly interprets the terms of those who are abandoned to suffering (οἱ καταλελειμμένοι καὶ οἱ ὀδυνώμενοι), and it is likely that the choice of words enables the translator to think of the diaspora of his own time.[2] The Peshitta understands verse 10 as a part of verse 9: 'The graven gods are

---

1 It is not clear (to me) how ibn Ezra takes this latter interpretation.
2 See Seeligmann, pp. 109, 113.

shattered'; it continues *b'r⁽ᵒ⁾ mn ḥsd wmn bly ᵓdr* (?) 'in the land for lack of harvest and threshing floor'.

The Targum expands the verse so as to present a simile: 'Kings who are skilful in waging war shall come against her to plunder her, even as the husbandman who is skilful at threshing grain',[1] by which presumably it seeks to portray Babylon as attacked (cf. rabbinic commentators above).

Rosenmüller and a number of modern scholars refer to Jer. li 33 where very similar phraseology is used of Babylon: 'The daughter of Babylon is like a threshing floor at the time when it is trodden' (R.V.). Delitzsch, however, urges caution in regard to the natural assumption that the comparison suggests Babylon as the object of the threshing in the present verse. For, as he says, 'Jeremiah has given a different turn to Isaiah's figure.' Rather Israel is alluded to (so e.g. Delitzsch, Procksch) as long oppressed and ill-treated (so e.g. Cheyne, *P.I.*, and Marti but with different oppressors in mind).

That the term בן גרני lit. 'son of my threshing-floor'[2] constitutes a synonym for מדשתי seems probable, and for this figurative use of the term בן, the phrases בְּנֵי רֶשֶׁף 'sparks' (Job v 7) and בֶּן־קָשֶׁת 'arrow' (Job xli 20) may be compared (cf. B.D.B., p. 121a 6). The phrase then denotes 'corn of my threshing-floor'. מדשתי is to be regarded with Procksch as an *abstractum pro concreto* and consequently its juxtaposition in the singular to לכם in the plural is intelligible and לכם need not be deleted as a secondary amplification of a shorter original (so Marti). The two synonyms then denote 'my threshed corn' and constitute a metaphor of a people subjected to oppression.[3]

The words מאת יהוה אלהי ישראל are taken by some modern commentators to be an editorial addition which has the function of making clear the source of the revelation of verses 9b and 10. There is something to be said for this view, for, as Wildberger observes, the parallelism of the verse is marred by its presence.

The sympathetic tone of the verse and of its phraseology most naturally indicates a reference to Israel or to the prophet's

---

1 For the Aramaic text, see Stenning.
2 Wildberger's insistence that the phrase means 'mein Tennensohn' rather than 'Sohn meiner Tenne' is otiose. No commentator, so far as I am aware, has wished to claim the opposite.
3 For which metaphor, cf. Mic. iv 12f and Isa. xli 15.

contemporaries rather than to Babylon (cf. Rosenmüller, D.K., Duhm, Marti, Procksch, Gray and Wildberger). Whether Israel was regarded as threshed by reason of the Babylonian exile or because she was caught up in the turmoils of the Assyrian domination of the east (so e.g. Cheyne, *P.I.*, and Erlandsson) depends on the view taken of the prophecy as a whole.

Verses 11 & 12

Verse 11a, מַשָּׂא דּוּמָה

As in Isa. xxi 1 and 13, and in xxii 1, the two words constitute the title of the oracle contained in verses 11f. All witnesses to the M.T. substantiate the reading except possibly the LXX which reads τὸ ὅραμα τῆς Ἰδουμαίας.[1] As has been shown (see on verse 1 above), the titles of the other oracles cited are derived from a word in the text. In this case, however, no word approximating in form to דומה is discernible in the text. The only word in the oracle with geographical import is מִשֵּׂעִיר 'from Seir' and as Seir denotes the land of Edom in Gen. xxxii 14 and Judg. v 4, it is reasonable to suppose that דומה denotes that same country. With such considerations in mind, and on the evidence of the LXX, some modern scholars have suggested that דומה is a corruption of an original אדום(ה).[2] On the other hand, the LXX's rendering may equally well be regarded as an interpretation of דומה. Thus, in P.T. *Ta'anith* 1:1 (p. 5) it is recorded in the name of R. Hanina ben R. Abahu that in R. Meir's book they found written 'the burden of Dumah' – 'the burden of Rome', משא דומה משה רומי.[3] It is possible that R. Meir wrote אדום as a marginal annotation, though it is more likely that he wrote רומי on the basis of the simple resemblance between ר and ד.[4] In any case, the tradition affords evidence of exegetical interpretation of דומה as אדם (or Rome) at a very early date.

Ibn Janah thinks דומה denotes 'the evil kingdom of Edom'. Under the root דיים ibn Janah compares the title of Isa. xxi 11

---

1 The word is simply transliterated by the Targum, Peshitta, Vulgate and Saadya.
2 So e.g. R. Lowth, Marti and, supposing 'ambivalence' (מַשָּׂא דוּמָ), I. O. Lehman.
3 The equation Edom = Rome was made by R. Aqiba; see *Bereshith Rabba* 65,21.
4 See J. P. Seigen, *The Severus Scroll and 1QIs*ᵃ, (Missoula, Mont., 1975), pp. 47f.

with Ezek. xxvii 32, מִי כְצוֹר כְּדֻמָה בְּתוֹךְ הַיָּם 'Who is there like Tyre, like her that is brought to silence in the midst of the sea?' (R.V.), and Ps. xciv 17, שָׁכְנָה דוּמָה נַפְשִׁי 'My soul had soon dwelt in silence' (R.V.). דומה then denotes 'destruction' (*hlkt*) and the title signifies 'the people doomed to destruction' (*ʾlʾmmt ʾlhlʾkt*).[1]

By contrast, ibn Ezra, followed by Qimhi, takes the view that דומה denotes an Arabian people and he refers to Gen. xxv 14 where דומה is listed as an offspring of Ishmael. Ibn Janah also notes this view and states that it may be intended by the Targum in that it leaves דומה untranslated. He is, however, dissatisfied with the suggestion because it does not accord with the reference to Seir (Edom) which so closely follows. Ibn Ezra attempts to resolve the problem by suggesting that the whole prophecy depicts a spy sent from Seir to search out Dumah. His suggestion is, however, unconvincing because it is fanciful and the details of it so involved that they defy comprehension.

Amongst modern commentators some follow ibn Janah's view that דומה is a figure of speech denoting Edom (so e.g. Rosenmüller, D.K., Duhm, Gray and Procksch), while others follow ibn Ezra in seeing in the word a reference to a people or city of that name (so e.g. Michaelis, Rabin, Wildberger). In connexion with this view two places with the name Dumah are attested, of which one only has been advocated as the Dumah of Isaiah xxi. First, there was a city of this name in the mountains of Judah mentioned in Jos. xv 52 and identified with modern Daume, south-west of Hebron.[2] It is unlikely, however, that a prophecy concerning a small Judaean town would find its place in the oracles of Isaiah (cf. D.K. and Wildberger). Secondly, there was the important city of North Africa named Dûmat-al-Jandal identified with the modern oasis el-Jôf. J. D. Michaelis was the first to argue that Isa. xxi 11f referred to this city, which is usually identified also with the offspring of Ishmael of Gen.

1 Similarly ben Bilam and Rashi. Ibn Janah thinks that Jerome may have left the word untranslated because he understood its 'secret' (i.e. that it signified 'destruction') and could not reproduce it in Latin.

2 See C. W. M. van der Velde, *Memoir* (Gotha, 1858), p. 308; cf. F.-M. Abel, *Géographie de Palestine*, II (3rd edn, Paris, 1967), pp. 308f. It is likely that Jerome's mention (commentary – see Migne) of a Dumah in Idumaea represents a confusion with this (Judaean) Dumah; at any rate, he is alone in mentioning such a place.

xxv 14.[1] The city is mentioned in Assyrian texts as *Adummu/utu*[2] and is not to be confused with *Udumu* (= Edom) which is also mentioned in such texts.

Verse 11b, אֵלַי קֹרֵא מִשֵּׂעִיר שֹׁמֵר מַה־מִּלַּיְלָה שֹׁמֵר מַה־מִלֵּיל

אלי קרא משעיר. The words are rendered by the LXX:[3] πρὸς ἐμὲ καλεῖ παρὰ τοῦ Σηιρ 'One is calling to me from Seir' with which the Vulgate agrees. The Targum is similar except that מן שמיא 'from heaven' appears as an interpretation of the M.T.'s משעיר (עלי אכלי מן שמיא – 'Unto me did one cry from heaven'). It is possible that אלי (interpreted secondarily as אֵלִי 'my God') may have influenced the Targum, for in P.T. *Taʾanith* 1:1 (p. 5)[4] R. Simon ben Yohai is said to have understood אלי קורא משעיר as 'My God calls to me from Seir' on the grounds that God was always present with Israel wherever they were exiled.

Rashi evidently follows this tradition with its double interpretation of אלי – 'The Holy One has said to me: the prophet or angel is calling to me because of the yoke of the kingdom of Edom.' It is possible too that it has influenced Qimhi who regards the voice of prophecy as the subject of the verb.

The Peshitta takes the watchman as the subject of the verb קרא and the later words מה מלילה מה מליל as an indication of the time at which the watchman was on duty: *ly qrʾ mn sᶜyr nṭwrʾ dbllyʾ* 'to me is calling from Seir the watchman that is (on duty) in the night'. The version is likely to represent a free and exegetical handling of the M.T. rather than as indicating a different text (cf. Goshen-Gottstein).

A different view is adopted by Saadya who translates אלי 'by עׄנא 'concerning us', taking (the people of) Dumah to be the subject of קרא 'Men ask about us from Mount Seir.'

The מן prefixed to שעיר is understood as מן of origin by all the ancient versions and rabbinic commentators except ibn

1 See B.D.B. For a more recent statement of this view, see Rabin.
2 For the identification, see M. Weippert in *W.O.* 7 (1973), 44n24. *Adumma/utu* was taken by Sennacherib in *c.* 691–689 B.C.
3 For the minor Greek versions, see below. There is some MS. evidence to suggest that the LXX (like the minor Greek versions) takes קרא as an imperative (e.g. καλειτε in A). Ottley, however, argues for the superiority of καλεῖ (indicative) – the reading of א, B and Q.
4 Cf. Schwab, p. 144. Jerome in his commentary mentions the possibility.

Janah and Rashi. משעיר denotes the place of origin of the call,
though for the minor Greek versions it denotes πρὸς ἐμὲ κάλει
τους φεύγοντας παρὰ τοῦ Σηείρ 'call to me those fleeing from
Seir'.[1]

Galling suggests that this reading presupposes that הַנֹּדְדִים
(or collectively הַנֹּדֵד) originally stood in the Hebrew text. Such
a view is, however, extremely unlikely; rather the rendering of
the minor Greek versions bears all the marks of an attempt to
clarify and elucidate the rendering of the LXX with which
substantially it is verbally identical (NB especially the use in
both of the preposition παρά).

Ibn Janah regards מן here as having the same force as the
preposition ל[2] and as meaning 'I heard one calling concerning
(ᶜn) Edom.' Rashi takes the מן as causative and renders 'The
prophet is calling to me [sc. God] because of the yoke of Edom
(מעול מלכות אדם).'

Modern translators and commentators are, however, virtually unanimous in giving to מן its usual sense of origin. The אלי
is taken to refer naturally to the prophet who hears in imagination the Seirites calling to him. As the words denote a visionary
or contrived image no difficulty need be seen in a Judaean
prophet hearing a voice from Edom or in a Judaean prophet
being consulted by foreigners[3] (even by Edomites!).

שמר. The massoretic pointing of the word as a participle with
the meaning 'watchman' is reflected in the ancient versions and
rabbinic commentators other than the LXX.[4] The latter
renders φυλάσσετε ἐπάλξεις 'guard the battlements' apparently understanding שמר as an imperative. The version continues
φυλάσσω τὸ πρώι καὶ τὴν νύκτα which differs widely from the
M.T.[5] as does the Targum with פריש להון ית נבואתא מא...
דעתיד למיתי 'O prophet, interpret unto them the prophecy,
what is to come.'

---

1 See Field, p. 645. Rabin adopts a similar view of משעיר: מי שבא|משעיר 'he who
  comes from Seir' (i.e. to Dumah).
2 See Neubauer, pp. 155f; ibn Janah cites Ex. xiv 3 and Ps. xxxi 12 as parallel
  instances.
3 So Delitzsch, D.K., Fohrer, Kaiser and Wildberger. Marti and Gray apparently
  think of an envoy of Edomite individuals travelling to Judah.
4 The Targum נביא 'O prophet' is interpretative.
5 It is possible that they read (אני) שמר את הבקר. See Goshen-Gottstein. For a
  discussion of the absence in the LXX of words corresponding to the last three
  words of the M.T. of this verse, see Ziegler, *Untersuchungen*, p. 48.

The view of the Targum that the watchman[1] is a figure for the prophet is generally assumed, though for Rashi the term denotes the guardian of Israel (i.e. God). The term שמר is usually compared with מצפה in verse 6, where the watchman denotes the prophet or the prophet's *alter ego*.[2] To this view P. Lohmann objects on the grounds that the word שֹׁמֵר (as opposed to צפה/מצפה) is not an O.T. designation of a prophet;[3] he concludes that the word means 'watchman' simply, and that the poem as a whole is a modification of an old (secular) watchman's song. Lohmann's view of the oracle as a whole must be considered later; here it is sufficient to note that his statement that שמר is not an O.T. designation for a prophet does not amount to grounds for denying that the specific denotation 'watchman' may be used as a figure for 'prophet'. For, as he himself admits, מצפה is widely so used. It should be noted also that the noun משמרת is used in verse 8 in close connexion with the מצפה (cf. Wildberger).

מה מלילה מה מליל. The words are taken to be an urgent question[4] addressed to the watchman. The מן prefixed to לילה (and ליל) is thought to mean 'concerning' by the Vulgate (*quid de nocte*) and by ibn Ezra, Rashi and Qimhi. For ibn Ezra the night is a particular night of the week and he refers to the night in which Moab was destroyed according to Isa. xv 1. For Rashi the night signifies the darkness and oppression suffered by Israel by reason of the yoke of Edom.

Saadya takes מן as partitive, and renders: כם מצי מן אלליל וכם בקי מנה 'How much of the night has elapsed and how much of it is still to come?' This latter interpretation of מן is adopted by virtually all modern commentators, though it should be noted here that it is rejected by ibn Ezra.[5]

The word ליל in the second half of the repeated question

---

1 For שמר with the meaning 'city watchman', see Song of Songs v 7.
2 So most modern commentators; see e.g. Marti and Procksch.
3 He discounts the late Isa. lxii 6 where שמרים denotes supernatural (angelic) beings.
4 Hence, according to e.g. Qimhi, Delitzsch, D.K., Wildberger, the repetition.
5 Rabin's view of the phrase is substantially the same as Saadya's, though he explicitly regards it as an Arabism. He observes that the phrase מה מלילה is unparalleled in biblical or later Hebrew literature and that the preposition מן in classical Arabic is commonly used to distinguish parts of the day or month. מה מלילה means 'what time is it?' 'what watch of the night is it?'

appears to be pointed as a construct. For this usage ibn Ezra refers to Isa. xv 1 (where the identical form occurs); he goes on to compare Song of Songs vii 10 with Ezek. xxvii 18; in the former text כְּיֵין הַטּוֹב omits the place of origin (in the absolute) of the wine, while in the latter (כְּיֵין חֶלְבּוֹן) the place is recorded. He deduces that a particular night – 'such and such a night of the week' – is intended (as in Isa. xv 1). Qimhi also notes that the form is a construct and he compares the phrase חֵיל כָּבֵד as it occurs in Isa. xxxvi 2. In fact these forms are best regarded as absolutes and as contractions of the normal forms חַיִל, לַיִל.[1]

As was indicated above, most modern scholars accept Saadya's view of the meaning of the question. On this view the image of the watchman is continued, and under the outward form of the normal question addressed to city (night) watchmen concerning the time of night,[2] the prophet is consulted by his questioners about their fate. Rashi's view that night here signifies the hard times of oppression is further supported by appeal to Mic. iii 6 and Isa. ix 1.[3]

One very different tradition concerning the words מלילה and מליל should be mentioned. According to P.T. *Taʾanith* 1:1 (p. 5),[4] שמר מה מליל is interpreted as if it read מה מילל[5] 'What did the watchman [*sc.* God] say?' It is probable that a similar tradition lies behind the addition in certain LXX manuscripts listed by Field (p. 465).[6] They read τί ὀλολύξεις φυλάσσων (τί ἀπὸ νυκτός;) 'What do you cry, O watchman? (What of the night?)' Here, however, the consonants were possibly read as a piel participle of the root ילל[7] 'to howl'.

These divergent traditions are best seen as arising from exegetical considerations rather than as indicating a variant Hebrew text. Thus, the P.T. account of the oracle clearly understood at least one set of the letters מהמליל in the sense given

---

1 Cf. G.K. 90f, 93w. For the view that the form is pausal, see e.g. Procksch.
2 Cf. e.g. D.K. and Lohmann, who cite Song of Songs iii 3; Pss. cxxi 3, cxxvii 1, cxxx 6.
3 So e.g. D.K. and Erlandsson; cf. Wildberger.
4 See Schwab, p. 144.
5 I.e. as third masculine singular piel perfect of the (Aramaic) word מלל (מִלֵּל) 'to speak'. Cf. Rabin, Hebrew, p. 242.
6 Cf. Ziegler's edn, p. 195. In *Untersuchungen* (p. 48) Ziegler raises the question whether the phrase is the original LXX reading at this point.
7 So Rabin, English, p. 303n3 and Goshen-Gottstein; cf. Wildberger.

to it by the Massoretes.[1] Further, the repetition itself was
(mis)understood as conveying the sense that the questioners
approached on two successive occasions. On the first occasion
they asked what was to come from the night, and on the second,
when Isaiah had had a chance to make enquiry, they asked
what the guardian of the world had said.

Verse 12, אָמַר שֹׁמֵר אָתָה בֹקֶר וְגַם לָיְלָה אִם־תִּבְעָיוּן בְּעָיוּ שֻׁבוּ אֵתָיוּ

אמר שמר. The words are deleted by Procksch *metri causa*,[2] and he
cites in support the absence of any word in the LXX which
corresponds to אמר and the fact that the prophet speaks of himself in the first person in verse 11. The LXX alone renders שמר
by a finite verb. Its φυλάσσω, however, hardly answers to an
Aramaism שָׁמֵר אֲנָא (so Procksch); it is more probable that it
read אֶשְׁמֹר (< שמר(א)מר). Procksch's argument that אמר שמר
should be deleted may be rejected; for considerations of metre
in so short an oracle are very far from certain, and his insistence
on consistency in the use of first or second person is out of place.

אתה בקר וגם לילה. With the exception of the LXX (on which,
see above), the words are taken as the watchman's answer to the
question of verse 11. The Vulgate and the Peshitta appear to
give a literal rendering: *venit mane, et nox/ʾtʾ ṣprʾ ʾp llyʾ* 'Morning
has come and night.' The Targum interprets day and night as
symbols of reward and punishment: 'There is a reward (אגר)
for the righteous and punishment or vengeance (פורענו) for the
wicked.' This interpretation is followed by the P.T.[3] which
states 'Morning for Israel, night for idolaters' and it recurs in
a number of modern commentators, e.g. Vitringa, Rosenmüller,
Delitzsch, Dillmann–Kittel.

Saadya gives to אתה a somewhat different meaning; he
renders: קד נהארכם וליילכם תקצי אגמעין 'Your day and your
night are both at an end.' In his notes on the text he paraphrases with לם יבק לכם יומא ולא לילה 'You have no longer day
or night.' It is likely that Saadya invests אתה with meanings

---

1 Thus מה יוצא לנו מתוך הלילה (p. 5). Cf. the LXX MSS. quoted above.
2 The line as a consequence has seven beats.
3 *Taʾanith* 1:1 (p. 5); cf. Schwab, p. 144.

attested rather for the Arabic cognate verb ʾty[1] than for Hebrew/
Aramaic אתא/אתה which means 'to come, to arrive' (see B.D.B.,
p. 86; Jastrow, p. 132).

Qimhi appears to know Saadya's interpretation, for he says
that some interpreters give the words the meaning: כבר נשלמו
הימים והלילות 'Already (Dumah's) days and nights are over'
(i.e. הגיע זמן קיצם 'The time of their end has arrived'). On the
other hand he himself is of the opinion that day and night are in
the future and indicate a period of respite (for Dumah) to be
followed by renewed attack against that town.

Modern commentators usually follow the more literal translations of the Vulgate and Peshitta, though there is some discrepancy about how the verb אתה (in the perfect tense) is
translated and some discussion about the force of וגם. The R.V.
renders the verb 'cometh' but notes in the margin as one
alternative 'is come'. N.E.B. has 'the morning comes'. Amongst
the commentators (e.g.) Ewald, Delitzsch, Cheyne (*P.I.*), Buhl,
Duhm, Kaiser and Fohrer assent to a present tense (in some
cases without referring to the problem) while Dillmann–Kittel,
Marti, Gray, Procksch and Wildberger indicate a perfect tense
(i.e. 'morning has come'). Dillmann–Kittel explicitly repudiate the view that the perfect אתה can properly be rendered by a
present tense, as does Procksch, though the latter scholar raises
the question whether the perfect is a prophetic perfect and
finally concludes with the suggestion that the verb is best read
as an (Aramaic) participle (אָתָא).

וגם is rendered simply *et* by the Vulgate (cf. Pesh.) and this is
followed by most modern commentators. F. Buhl,[2] however,
gives to the expression a concessive force: 'Morning comes even
if it is also night (wenn es auch Nacht ist)' on the grounds that
this alone makes sense of the watchman's answer. Marti and
Procksch both reject this translation on the grounds that it is
doubtful, the latter suggesting that the absence of a verb makes
it particularly so. On the other hand גַּם כִּי is attested with
concessive force[3] and, as גם alone is so used in Isa. xlix 15, it is

---

1 'To complete conclude, terminate (active)' – Wehr, p. 3. Lane, p. 16, quotes
  the phrase أتى عليه حول 'a year passed over him'.
2 *Geschichte der Edomiter* (Leipzig, 1893), pp. 68ff. More recently he has been
  followed by Kaiser.
3 See B.D.B., p. 169b 6, and G.K. 160.

not unreasonable to suppose that וגם was capable of bearing this meaning. It seems to me that the real difficulty with Buhl's view is that he renders אתה by a present tense for which there is no justification (so Wildberger). If a past tense is substituted – 'morning has come, even if it still be night' – the result is non-sensical even if interpreted symbolically of salvation and oppression.

Procksch believes that a verb is missing from the phrase וגם הלילה. On this assumption, and comparing Isa. xviii 5, he proposes to read וגמל לילה 'the night is complete', assuming further that the ל of וגמל has dropped out by haplography. The proposal is, however, to be rejected; first, there is no evidence for such an emendation and, secondly, גמל is not elsewhere predicated of times or seasons in the sense of 'be full, complete'. In Isa. xviii 5 it denotes grapes that are ripe.

Two other modern scholars also consider that a verb should be predicated of לילה as אתה is of בקר. A. Scheiber[1] and Rabin, apparently independently, see such a verb in גם with which they compare Arabic ǧmm 'to be full'. Rabin notes that the Arabic word is used of wells, measures etc. and suggests that in this verse the same verb might indicate that a period of time is full (i.e. complete) in the way attested for the verb מלא. Scheiber admits that such a verb גמם does not occur elsewhere in the bible, though Rabin (in *V.T.* 5 (1955), 154) finds another instance in the obscure Hab. i 9,[2] 'their faces are sappy with burning wind (i.e. full, as with liquid)'. The translations of Isa. xxi 12 offered by both scholars are the same: 'The day has come, the night is full (i.e. completed)', i.e. the period of oppression is over.

The suggestion is attractive[3] in that it gives, without emendation, the more obvious meaning previously sought by Procksch. In Rabin's case it is also consistent with his view that the oracle is replete with Arabisms. On the other hand, according to Lane, Arabic ǧmm properly denotes (of water) 'it *became much* or *abundant* or it *collected*' and (of a measure) 'it *became full* or *filled*'.[4]

---

1 In *V.T.* 11 (1961), 455. He approves the sense gained by Procksch's emendation though not the emendation itself.

2 B.D.B., p. 169.

3 It is mentioned as a conjecture by K.B.(3), p. 190, and recorded as an alternative in the margin of the N.E.B.

4 Wehr gives 'to gather'. B.D.B. compare the Hebrew particle with this Arabic word.

There is, it seems to me, no evidence that the word could properly be predicated of periods of time, and to assume for the word, as Rabin does, the same usage as is attested for Hebrew מלא involves a considerable degree of speculation including the supposition (to which Rabin freely admits) that Isaiah is 'employing an unusually high degree of stylistic artificiality'.

That the author of the oracle should have used so unusual a verb when מלא and (Arabic) *ml^ɔ* would more readily have conveyed in Hebrew and Arabic the meaning 'to be full' is most unlikely. There is, moreover, no support for such a view of וגם either in the ancient versions or in the rabbinic commentators (including significantly those who wrote in Arabic).

אם תבעיון בעיו. The LXX, Vulgate and Peshitta all follow the M.T. closely, though the LXX has singular verbs (ἐὰν ζητῆς ζήτει). The Targum reproduces the conditional sentence but its verb תוב clearly answers to the M.T.'s שובו rather than to the phrase תבעיון בעיו which is not reproduced; אם תיבין אתון תובו 'If ye will repent, repent.' The Peshitta renders the verb בעה by the Syriac cognate *b^{cɔ}* and the Vulgate by *quaero* 'to seek, ask, enquire'. Ibn Ezra observes that the word בעה is of Aramaic origin and that the third radical yodh (י for ה) is included in both forms.[1] He gives to the words the meaning 'to seek' or 'desire' (בקש). It is not entirely clear (to me) what he means by the paraphrase אם תבקשו לבוא בקשו but he probably intends 'If you desire to come, (you may) desire' (i.e. it is permitted).[2]

Saadya renders: פאי מטלב טלבתמוה 'No matter what may be the quest you have entered upon (turn back from it and approach).' In his notes he gives the following paraphrase: פארגעו מן אלחרב אלתי כנתם קצדתמוהא 'Turn back from the war which you were intending (to prosecute).' He notes that the two words תבעיו בעיו are Aramaic and he compares with them Dan. vi 8, כָּל־דִּי יִבְעֵה בָעוּ ('Whosoever shall ask a petition' (R.V.)). By his comparison with this phrase, Saadya probably intends to indicate that he takes the word בעיו in Isa. xxi 12 as the cognate noun בָּעוּ which follows the verb (תבעיון) in the accusative, for his translation is consistent with this supposition.

The Aramaic word בעא properly denotes 'to seek, ask for,

---

1 1QIs^a has the forms without the yodh.
2 Friedländer renders: 'If you wish to come, do so.'

pray'[1] and with this Saadya's choice of the word *ṭlb* as a translation appears to agree. On the other hand, in his paraphrase he gives to the words the particular meaning 'to seek (to prosecute) a war'.[2]

Another military use of בעה is attested in Obad. 6, and ibn Janah, in his comments on the root בעה, compares Isa. xxi 12 with this verse. Here the niphal of בעה is found in parallelism with the niphal of חפש‎: אֵיךְ נֶחְפְּשׂוּ עֵשָׂו נִבְעוּ מַצְפֻּנָיו 'See how Esau's treasure is ransacked, his secret wealth hunted out!' (N.E.B.; cf. R.V.: 'How are his hidden treasures sought up!'). The word בעה here plainly indicates that Edom's wealth was 'exposed and plundered' at the hands of Edom's enemies (see B.D.B. under חפש).

Reference to the Arabic cognate word *bġy* may be held to substantiate such hostile meanings for the root בעה.[3] As well as '*he sought diligently*', Lane gives for the word '*he acted injuriously or wrongfully* or *tyranically*' and for the phrase بغى عليه '*he exalted himself against him*' '*overpowered* or *oppressed him*'. Dozy, moreover, notes the meaning 'demander avec arrogance' for the same word.[4]

Rabin,[5] who notes Saadya's interpretation of the verse, is inclined to see behind תבעיון (but not in בעיו) the rare Arabic word *bᶜw* which he thinks means 'to attack' as well as 'to sin'.[6] The word *bᶜw* is attested in Old South Arabian, and given the meaning 'to commit a crime or treason' by A. Jamme (p. 85). Rabin, in his English article, questions whether such a meaning fits the contexts of the relevant South Arabian texts and then, because the word is attested with the meaning 'to borrow a

---

1 See B.D.B., p. 1085; cf. Jastrow, p. 181. Syriac *bᶜᵓ* has similar meanings.

2 Ibn Ezra in his paraphrase also seems to allude to a military expedition; it is clear from the context that 'to come' in the phrase אם תבקשו לבוא בקשו has a military connotation.

3 A hostile sense for Aramaic בעא in the early Aramaic inscriptions is also listed by Hoftijzer, p. 40.

4 Ibn Barun explicitly compares בעה in Isa. xxi 12 with Arabic *bġy*, though Wechter offers the English translations 'to request, desire'. It is doubtful, however, whether *bġy* can mean 'request'. Gesenius–Buhl hold the theory that 'overpass the mark, swell up' is the fundamental meaning of the root בעה/*bġy*. Cf. Donner and Röllig, II, glossary.

5 For Rabin's complete translation of the Dumah oracle, see below, p. 80.

6 Belot gives for *bᶜᵓ* 'commettre un délit'; the word is not listed by Lane, Dozy or Wehr.

riding animal' (which, Rabin supposes, denotes part of the preparations for war), he posits for it the extended meaning 'attack'.[1] Rabin's argument is unconvincing by reason of the considerable degree of supposition that is necessary to achieve such a meaning for what is (as he admits) a rare word. I am not competent to enter into discussions of the Old South Arabian evidence, but I may be permitted to comment that Rabin not only claims for b^cw the meaning 'attack', but also for $b\dot{g}$ in the Thamudic phrase $slm\ b\dot{g}$[2] in which he thinks the second word is a form of $b\dot{g}y$.[3] If, then, he thinks Arabic $b\dot{g}y$ (i.e. with $\dot{g}$) is capable of the meaning 'attack', it is not necessary to posit for Saadya's understanding of Isa. xxi 12 that תבעיון is cognate with a rare Arabic word b^cw; it is enough to suggest that it reflects the well-attested root $b\dot{g}y$ (see above). With this conclusion also the M.T., which has a yodh between the ע and the ו of תבעיון, is consistent.

It is convenient here to consider also Rabin's view of the word בעיו. In common with the Targum, Vulgate and Peshitta, he takes the word to be an imperative and he gives to it the meaning 'to pray' which is well attested for Aramaic בעא. He considers that the word is here cognate with Arabic $b\dot{g}y$, which, in his English article, he says means 'to desire, to ask for'. In his Hebrew article, however, he appears to give to the Arabic word the meaning 'to pray'. He renders the phrase as a whole: 'If you have sinned/attacked, pray.'[4] The conditional structure of the phrase matches the conditional phrase (compounded of two imperatives) which then follows: 'If you repent, you will go home' (for details of this, see below).

Again difficulties are presented by Rabin's analysis. First, that the two words of the phrase should represent two different roots, while possible, is surely unlikely.[5] Secondly, it seems to be necessary to Rabin's argument that the words should be couched at least in 'pseudo-Arabicized Hebrew'.[6] בעיו with the meaning that Rabin seeks for it might be characterized as Aramaicized

---

1 In his Hebrew article he states more boldly (but without any references) that it is used many times of a raid or a sudden attack. See Hebrew, p. 249.
2 Branden, p. 418. He gives it the meaning 'vaincre'.
3 Rabin, English, p. 308n21a.
4 As frequently in the Talmud, 'pray' means 'implore mercy'; cf. Jastrow, p. 181.
5 Cf. also Isaiah's אם לא תאמינו כי לא תאמנו where the same root is used. Isa. vii 9.
6 His actual phrase, used in an analogy, is 'pseudo-Italianized English'.

Hebrew with talmudic overtones, but it cannot be *Arabicized* Hebrew. For *bġy*, while certainly capable of the meaning 'to desire', is not attested, so far as I am aware, with the meaning 'to pray' and certainly not with the extended meaning 'to implore mercy'.

One other modern interpretation of the phrase in question should be noted. H. Winckler[1] considers that in Job iii 5 a form of the verb בעה is paralleled by the word גאל and he consequently posits for the verb בעה the meaning 'to help'.[2] The whole phrase of Isa. xxi 12 אם תבעיו בעה שובו אתיו (*sic*) then means 'If you really wish to help, then occupy your place on my side.' Winckler's view may be rejected. He adduces no philological evidence to support his theory; nor does he show why the verb in Job iii 5 should not be taken as a form of the root בעת as is customary.

Among the rabbinic scholars Qimhi paraphrases the forms of בעה by using the verb שאל 'to ask, enquire'. He interprets the phrase (as a conditional imperfect followed by an imperative) to mean that the enquirer will wish to ask again by reason of the continued threat of the enemy which is implied by the symbol of night following dawn.

Qimhi's view that the meaning of בעה is שאל 'ask, enquire' is almost universally adopted by modern commentators and translators.[3] In conjunction with the words שובו אתיו which follow, the words are taken to indicate that because an ambiguous answer has been given by the prophet, the enquirers are free to return to pose again their question.

However, as Rabin properly remarks, it is very doubtful whether בעה can bear the meaning 'enquire, ask'. For, as he says, in biblical Aramaic בעא never means 'to enquire, ask a question' and in Targum Onkelos to the Pentateuch בעא answers to Hebrew בקש 'request, seek' and never to שָׁאַל (for which שְׁאֵל is reserved). Further, on the view that this oracle is early, no instance is cited by Hoftijzer for בעא with the sense 'ask, enquire' in early Aramaic inscriptions; rather he lists

---

1 *Altorientalische Forschungen*, vol. III (Leipzig, 1902), pp. 218ff.
2 He emends (by reference to the LXX) Job xxx 24 to find another instance of the verb in this sense.
3 E.g. R.V., N.E.B., Hitzig, Delitzsch, Cheyne (*P.I.*), D.K., Duhm, Marti, Gray, Kaiser, Fohrer, Wildberger.

'vouloir, désirer, chercher'. We may add that B.D.B., K.B. and K.B.[(3)] cite Isa. xxi 12 alone as an instance for בעה 'enquire, fragen'.[1]

שבו אתיו. The two words are taken as imperatives by the M.T., Vulgate (*convertimini*, *venite*) and by the rabbinic and modern commentators. The LXX's παρ' ἐμοὶ οἴκει appears to reflect a reading of the verb ישב rather than of שוב and παρ' ἐμοί answers, perhaps, to אֵתִי rather than to אתיו (see Goshen–Gottstein). The Peshitta renders שובו by the adverb *twb* 'again' and אתיו by a participial form (with pronoun) '*tytwn*.[2] The Targum has '(If you will repent, repent) while ye can repent' (דאתון יכלין למתב where אתון may indicate that it read אתיו in this way).

Ibn Ezra interprets the words more physically: 'If you wish to come, you may – return to those that sent you and come all together' (*sc.* as a military expedition).[3] For Saadya the phrase means ארגעו ענה ואקבלו 'desist from (your military quest) and approach', though unfortunately his notes do not make clear what he intended by 'approach'.

As has been indicated above most modern commentators interpret the words (taken with אם תבעיו בעיו) to indicate an assurance to the prophet's questioners that they may return later for a more definite answer if they so wish. 'If ye will inquire, inquire, come again' (so e.g. R.V., margin).

Delitzsch is inclined to see a secondary meaning in שובו, i.e. 'to repent', and to this extent he follows the Targum and the Vulgate (cf. Rashi). Dillmann–Kittel and Duhm, however, repudiate this view on syntactical grounds (D.K.)[4] or as being inconsistent with the function of the prophet of the oracle (Duhm).

Rabin has revived the idea that שובו here denotes 'repent' in a religious sense. For אתיו, however, he compares Ethiopic *atawa* with the particular sense 'to return home' (either to one's house or country) and he posits precisely this meaning for אתיו in

---

1 It is likely that the Vulgate's *si quaeritis, quaerite* has considerably influenced Western translations and commentators. For *quaero* in Latin means 'to ask, enquire' as well as 'to seek'.

2 I.e. *Si quaesituri estis, quaerite, tum demum venietis.* So Walton, III, *ad loc.* Cf. the grammatically identical but variant '*tyn* '*ntwn* cited by Diettrich.

3 Qimhi's alternative interpretation.

4 I.e. because 'repent' and 'come', even if asyndetically coupled, do not make sense when juxtaposed.

the present verse.[1] The two imperatives שׁוּבוּ אֵתָיוּ constitute a conditional clause (cf. G.K. 110f) with the meaning 'If you repent, then you will return' (i.e. home) or 'repent, that you may return'.

The difficulty with Rabin's view is that he invests אֵתָיוּ with a meaning which is attested only in Ethiopic and (possibly) in Old South Arabian, but not in Hebrew, Aramaic or Arabic (cf. the standard Arabic–English lexica). Even on Rabin's view that the author is making use of Arabicized Hebrew, it is surely implausible that he should make use of a word widely attested in Semitic speech but with a special meaning attested only in Ethiopic and (possibly) in South Arabian and for which there is no supporting evidence in the ancient versions or rabbinic commentators.

Another possibility for the word אֵתָיוּ may be posited by reference to its two other occurrences in the book of Isaiah. In lvi 9 and 12 the identical imperative plural form is found complete with the radical yodh.[2] In lvi 12 the plural imperative is immediately followed by a first person singular verb: אֶקְחָה אֵתָיוּ יַיִן 'Come ye, *say they*, I will fetch wine' (R.V.). It is probable that the word is used here merely as a stereotyped interjection just as the imperatives הבה, לכה etc. are also used without concord in this way.[3] That in lvi 9 the same imperative does still express an independent idea (viz. 'Come to eat') does not militate against this view as e.g. לְכוּ/לְכָה are also clearly used sometimes in this way. On this view אֵתָיוּ in Isa. xxi 12 expresses merely encouragement like English 'Come now...'

Verses 13–15

Verse 13a, מַשָּׂא בַּעְרָב

Except for the LXX, which has no corresponding words,[4] all witnesses to the M.T. substantiate its reading.[5] The words are

---

1 He quotes also as evidence Old South Arabian ᵓtw 'to return' and, tentatively, Thamudic ᵓty in the same sense. (He notes that Branden gives to the word the meaning 'est venu (ici)', i.e. to arrive.) It is not clear to me how these words substantiate the specific meaning 'come *home*'.

2 For this form, see G.K. 29t and 75u. Ibn Ezra notes the irregular tsere for hateph-pathaḥ beneath the aleph and suggests that the pointing arises from the guttural character of aleph.

3 Cf. G.K. 105b.

4 On this, see Ziegler, *Untersuchungen*, p. 48.

5 The Peshitta does not reproduce the beth, having simply: mšqlᵓ dᶜrbyᵓ. (The readings dᶜrbᵓ and dᶜrb are attested; for which, see Diettrich.)

taken as the title to the prophecy contained in verses 13–17 and the title is derived from the keyword בערב as it occurs in the text of verse 13 (cf. on xxi 1). In the text of verse 13, the M.T. reads בַּעְרַב, though the ancient versions understand the consonants here to denote בָּעֶרֶב 'in the evening'. The versions and commentators are, however, unanimous in understanding בערב in the title to refer to the Arabs or Arabia rather than to 'evening'.[1] As the title merely reproduces a keyword from the text and so labels the oracle (i.e. The Oracle בערב), Qimhi's attempt to give to ב the same meaning as על 'concerning' is otiose.

Verse 13b, בַּיַּעַר בַּעְרַב תָּלִינוּ אֹרְחוֹת דְּדָנִים׃

The word תלינו is taken as an imperfect or jussive by all the ancient versions and commentators,[2] though the LXX and Targum have for the M.T.'s second person plural the third person singular and third person plural respectively. The LXX, by so doing, appears to link verse 13 with verse 12 and to regard the verb (κοιμηθήσῃ) as an amplification of the phrase παρ' ἐμοὶ οἴκει (for which, see above).

ארחות דדנים is generally understood as a vocative following the second person plural verb (e.g. 'you caravans of Dedan' – N.E.B.), though in the Targum it is the subject of the third person plural verb and in the LXX (ἐν τῇ ὁδῷ Δεδαν) (ארח)ות) is taken as a form of אֹרַח 'path' rather than as the plural of the noun אֹרְחָה 'caravan'.[3] The phrase ארחות דדנים refers to the caravans of the well-known merchant tribe who, according to Ezek. xxv 13, lived in north-west Arabia on the southern boundary of Edom, though according to Gen. x 7 they were further to the south.[4]

A different view of the words תלינו ארחות דדנים is taken by Saadya. For him the word דדנים alone is vocative and ארחות is

---

1 The versions and Massoretes probably intended 'Against Arabia or the Arabs'.
2 Amongst moderns, e.g. Delitzsch, Duhm, Gray, Kaiser, Fohrer see the word as a jussive.
3 B.D.B., p. 73b, mentions the possibility that the word ארחות 'caravans' may be derived from ארח 'path' by metonymy; cf. ibn Janah's view: رفاق مارّة السبل 'caravans which traverse the path'.
4 See further W. F. Albright, in G. Ebeling (ed.), *Geschichte und Altes Testament* (Alt Festschrift, Tübingen, 1953), pp. 1ff.

to be rendered אציאפכם 'your guests', whereby he understands the word as a qal participle form of the verb elsewhere used in this sense in Jer. ix 1.[1] תלינו is rendered as if it were a hiphil (יכון תביתון) and the phrase as a whole is taken to mean 'is it a good[2] thing that you should make your guests pass the night in the scrub?'

ביער. The word is rendered 'in the forest' or 'thicket' by the ancient versions (δρυμῷ, *saltu*, חורשא, ‘*bʾ*). The translation 'forest' is, of course, quite unsuited to the context (cf. Delitzsch). Saadya uses the word שערי (*šʿry*) which denotes 'scrub country'. Delitzsch draws attention to the Arabic cognate root *wʿr* which is used properly in the sense 'rocky terrain', though such terrain was also sometimes planted with trees which furnished fire-wood. Wehr gives for the noun the meaning 'covered with rock, debris, rugged, wild, rough, roadless' and we may confidently assert that the word יער in this text denotes the harsh desert in which the fugitives are to spend the night.

As has been indicated above, בערב is read by all the ancient versions as the noun עֶרֶב 'evening'. This interpretation is noted by Qimhi, though he seems to prefer the alternative 'Arabia'. Saadya renders by אחסן 'is it good?', presumably deriving ערב from the root ערב III 'to be sweet, pleasing' (see B.D.B., p. 787), and interpreting בערב adverbially.

Some commentators (e.g. Lowth, Michaelis, Rosenmüller, Hitzig) adopt the reading בָּעֶרֶב 'in the evening' on the grounds that it fits the context admirably and avoids the otherwise harsh asyndetical 'in the forest, in Arabia'.[3] More recently, however, it has been usual to retain the pointing of the M.T. and to reject the tradition of the versions.[4] Thus, D.K., Duhm, Marti and Wildberger all reject the reading בָּעֶרֶב 'in the evening' on the grounds that it is superfluous with the verb תלינו. The argument is hardly an impressive one. Admittedly the English phrase 'in the evening pass the night' (cf. German 'übernachten/die Nacht zubringen') appears tautologous, but לון includes in its semantic range the meaning 'lodge, encamp'

---

1 He explains the feminine ending as a mere variant like שנות שנים.
2 For this translation, see under בערב below.
3 The same harshness led Marti to the view that ביער was a corrupt dittograph of בערב.
4 Delitzsch thinks both traditions are correct and that as Dumah in the preceding oracle has two senses, so here does ערב.

and this conjoined with 'in the evening' gives a meaning which is entirely appropriate.

Because the word ערב is not attested elsewhere in the O.T. with the sense 'Arabia', and also because ב does not elsewhere follow משא ('oracle') in the sense 'against', a number of scholars have followed Ewald in seeing in בערב the meaning 'in the steppe, desert'. Ewald asserts that this is the original meaning of the word which only later came to be used to characterize the steppe-dwellers or Arabs.[1] The word, however, does not occur elsewhere in this sense,[2] which is conveyed rather by the feminine noun ערבה (B.D.B., p. 787b (4 and 5)). Further, there is no versional or early Jewish tradition to support such a meaning for the word in this verse. The noun ערב in the bible properly denotes the Arabs or steppe-dwellers of North Arabia (cf. Wiseman, *Peoples*, p. 289) and consequently the N.E.B. (so, hesitantly, Gray) is probably accurate when, taking the massoretic view of the pointing, it renders: '(You caravans of Dedan, that camp in the scrub) with the Arabs'.[3]

For Saadya's taking the verse as a question, see on verse 15 below.

Verse 14, לִקְרַאת צָמֵא הֵתָיוּ מָיִם יֹשְׁבֵי אֶרֶץ
תֵּימָא בְּלַחְמוֹ קִדְּמוּ נֹדֵד:

The interpretation of this verse turns largely on the way in which the verbs התיו and קדמו are taken. The massoretic pointing of the former verb is ambiguous in that it may indicate either an imperative or a perfect.[4] The latter verb, however, is pointed as a perfect and consequently it is natural to assume that התיו was taken as a perfect by the Massoretes (cf. G.K. 76d).

The ancient versions, on the other hand, are unanimous in taking both verbs as imperatives, with the natural consequence that ישבי ארץ תימא is understood as a vocative. A number of

---

1 The shift in meaning took place, according to Ewald, not before the seventh century B.C. and is first attested in Jer. iii 2 and Ezek. xxvii 21.
2 D.K. and Wildberger, who adopt Ewald's view, admit as much.
3 Cf. Rashi and ibn Ezra's paraphrases of the title על ערביים (Rashi), עלّ ערב, והם בני קדר (ibn Ezra). Similarly Saadya renders the title: קצّה פי אלאעראב 'The prophecy about the Arabs'.
4 Jer. xii 9 contains the same form where the context clearly indicates an imperative; cf. G.K. 68i.

modern commentators[1] adopt this view of the verse on the grounds that it can, as a consequence, be brought into relation with verse 13, and because the imperfect תלינו in verse 13 cannot be harmonized with perfects in verse 14. Accordingly they emend the pointing of the second verb to read קָדְמוּ.

Amongst the rabbinic commentators, Saadya also regards the two verses as connected. Verse 14 continues the question posed in verse 13: '(Is it good)...that you offer food to the fugitive without coming to meet the thirsty with water?' In his notes on this passage Saadya states that he understands the prophecy as a whole to refer by allusion (באלאשארה) to the incident mentioned in *P.T. Ta'anith* iv.[2] The passage, which in turn refers to Isa. xxi 13f, relates that 80,000 young men of the priesthood fled through Nebuchadrezzar's lines to the Ishmaelites; the latter, when asked for refreshment, gave the refugees only a species of salt plant and leather skins full of air with the unfortunate result that one of them choked and died (for Saadya the number who died has swollen to 80,000).[3]

It is likely that this particular interpretation of the prophecy has led Saadya to adapt his translation of the Hebrew text accordingly. Apart from the question of the meanings he gives to the words (and some are at least possible), there is nothing in the Hebrew text to justify his rendering the first half of verse 14 in a negative or privative sense, i.e. 'without coming to meet the fugitive with water...' (מן דון אן).

It is possible that the tradition to which Saadya refers has influenced the massoretic pointing of קָדְמוּ (i.e. as a perfect), for thereby reference to the incident mentioned is facilitated.

Another view of the relationship between verses 13 and 14 is presented by Gray, who adopts the pointing of the M.T. for the verbs of verse 14. He regards verse 13 as fragmentary and the words in it ארחות דדנים as parallel to ישבי ארץ תימא and as marking the beginning of the couplet:

> The caravans of the Dedanites to meet the thirsty
> brought water,

<ol>
<li>So e.g. Rosenmüller, Cheyne (P.I.), D.K., Duhm, Marti, Procksch, Kaiser, Wildberger.</li>
<li>P. 43; cf. Schwab, pp. 192f. An expanded form of the same story occurs in Midrasch Echa Rabbati, ed. S. Buber (Wilna, 1899), II, 4, p. 22a.</li>
<li>Rashi in his comments also refers to this story.</li>
</ol>

> The inhabitants of the land of Temaʾ met the
> fugitives with bread.

The reconstruction is attractive but it should be noted that Gray can make virtually nothing of the remainder of the words of verse 13.

Kissane follows Gray in understanding 'caravans of Dedanites' as parallel to 'inhabitants of the land of Temaʾ'. For him, though, the first words of verse 13 constitute a relative clause in apposition to ארחות דדנים which follows: 'Ye that abide in a forest in the steppe, ye caravans of Dedanites...' The verbs which follow are taken as imperatives and the fugitives are the tribe of Kedar.

Kissane's treatment of the verse is an improvement on Gray's and his understanding of the syntax, though perhaps somewhat strained,[1] is possible. On the other hand, it is strange on his view that no indication is given of the identity of the fugitives until verses 16f.

תימא is the important place in the Hejaz in north-west Arabia (modern Teyma) which was famous for its water supply (for literature, see B.D.B., p. 1066). In Gen. xxv 15 Teima is listed as the ninth son of Ishmael, and in Jer. xxv 23 תימא and דדן are again found juxtaposed.

The LXX renders by Θαιμαν and the other ancient versions by 'austri', דרומא and *tymn*ʾ. It is most unlikely that the LXX read תימן in this verse, as Θαιμαν occurs also in the LXX of Gen. xxv 15 and Jer. xxv 23. Kocherus's[2] analysis of the treatment of both תימא and תימן by the ancient versions suggests that the LXX used Θαιμαν indifferently to render תימא and תימן. While the other versions generally understood תימא to be a proper name they occasionally confuse it (as here) with תימן; for this latter is translated by them in a number of places as 'South' (i.e. from the root ימן).[3]

בלחמו. The third person singular suffix is usually understood to refer to the fugitive, i.e. the bread that he needs.[4] The suffix

---

1 He cites no other instance of a relative clause preceding a subject to which it refers.

2 See Rosenmüller, pp. 487f. I have not had access to Kocherus's work.

3 T. Nöldeke, in *Encyclopaedia Biblica*, I, ed. J. S. Black and T. K. Cheyne, under the entry 'Ishmael' thinks that תימא and תימן are synonyms; the former is derived from a root ימא with the meaning 'South'.

4 Cf. Rosenmüller, Delitzsch, Wildberger, etc.

is not translated by the LXX and Vulgate, but this does not amount to evidence that it was not before them. The Peshitta has a second masculine plural suffix (*lḥmkwn*) with which the Targum appears to agree: מְמָא דָאַתוּן אָכְלִין ' (prepare) what you are eating'. These again are best regarded as legitimate (if free) renderings of the M.T. rather than evidence for a different text.

Verse 15, כִּי־מִפְּנֵי חֲרָבוֹת נָדָדוּ מִפְּנֵי חֶרֶב נְטוּשָׁה וּמִפְּנֵי קֶשֶׁת דְּרוּכָה וּמִפְּנֵי כֹּבֶד מִלְחָמָה:

The verse seems to indicate the cause of the flight of the refugees. The repetition of מִפְּנֵי together with the listed weapons depicts sharply the overwhelming nature of the danger from which they flee (so e.g. Delitzsch).

כִּי at the beginning of the verse is best taken as 'for' with the Targum and Peshitta and Vulgate rather than as asseverative. The LXX renders מפני each time by διὰ τὸ πλῆθος which may represent a misreading of חרב as רב (multitude) or מרבית (abundance).[1]

Amongst modern scholars Kissane has sought to avoid repetition of the word 'sword' by repointing the M.T.'s חֲרָבוֹת 'swords' as חֳרָבוֹת 'desolations'. There is, however, no evidence to support his proposal. Further, as the word חָרְבָּה denotes ruins (e.g. of a city) it hardly fits the context in which men are said to flee from the weapons and press of war.

חרב נטושה. The passive participle נטושה is rendered שְׁלִיפָא 'drawn' by the Targum. Rosenmüller approves this meaning, citing the Talmudic word נטש with the meaning 'to skin (an animal)'.[2] The Peshitta renders *ltyšᵓ* 'sharpened, polished' with which Saadya's סיף מצקול 'sharpened sword' may be compared. Ibn Ezra, probably referring to Saadya's version, states that some authorities regard נטושה as a by-form of לטושה, the nun and the lamedh being interchangeable.[3] A number of modern commentators adopt this view of the word, or mention it but prefer to think that נטושה is in fact a scribal mistake for לטושה.[4]

1 See Ottley, p. 209. 1QIs^a reads רבות for חרבות which may (but Goshen-Gottstein thinks not) reflect the same tradition.
2 For this word, see B.D.B., p. 643. On this view it would be more appropriate to cite Isa. xxxiii 23 where the word is used of slack (i.e. loosed) rigging.
3 Cf. Rashi (who cites the parallel נִשְׁכָּה for לִשְׁכָּה in Neh. xiii 7) and ben Bilam, p. 69.
4 Cf. e.g. Marti, Gray, Procksch, Kissane.

A different view of the word is suggested by ibn Janah, who is followed by ibn Ezra, Rashi and Qimhi. He compares the phrase predicated of the Amalekites in 1 Sam. xxx 16, נטושים על־פני כל הארץ, and renders the word נטושים by *mnbsṭwn* 'they were spread out (over all the ground)'.[1] The meaning of מחרב נטושה is, as Qimhi makes plain, that the fugitives flee from the swords which are spread abroad (פשטה) in their land.

קשת דרוכה lit. 'the trodden bow', the bow which has been strung ready for battle. It does not indicate the bow bent by the archer's drawing back the string prior to shooting.[2]

כבד המלחמה. The noun is used of a storm in Isa. xxx 27. Here it seems to indicate vehemence, force.

Verses 16 & 17

כִּי כֹה אָמַר אֲדֹנָי אֵלָי בְּעוֹד שָׁנָה כִּשְׁנֵי

שָׂכִיר וְכָלָה כָּל־כְּבוֹד קֵדָר: וּשְׁאָר מִסְפַּר־קֶשֶׁת

גִּבּוֹרֵי בְנֵי־קֵדָר יִמְעָטוּ כִּי יְהוָה אֱלֹהֵי יִשְׂרָאֵל דִּבֵּר:

The verses are similar in form and language to Isa. xvi 14. 1QIs^a reads שלוש שנים for the M.T.'s שנה and this may constitute evidence that שלש was lost by homoioarkton. The reading is adopted by Kaiser who notes that the figure has 'long been noticed as missing'. Earlier, Duhm, followed by Marti, compared Isa. xvi 14 where the number three does occur and consequently they supposed that the prophet here left a space for the number until he could be sure what it should be. In support of their supposition they draw attention to 1 Sam. xiii 1 where a number has dropped out and to the plural phrase כשני שכיר which, they argue, follows awkwardly in the M.T. upon a single year.

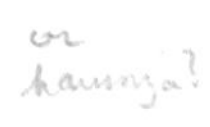

Fundamentally, the argument of Duhm and Marti rests upon the supposition that, because the phrase כשני שכיר is awkward if it follows a single year, a higher number ought to be present in the text. Their fundamental assumption is, however, far from axiomatic. The phrase from בעוד to שכיר is rendered by Saadya 'In a year counted as the years of a hireling' (i.e. exactly; cf. N.E.B.) which indicates the possibility that כשני שכיר was a

---

1 Rashi cites also 1 Sam. v 18, and Qimhi, Judg. xv 9.
2 See J. A. Emerton in *J.T.S.* n.s. 27 (1976), 391f.

stereotyped phrase with this particular meaning. That the phrase occurs in identical form but after 'three years' in Isa. xvi 14 is also consistent with this view of it. Similarly, the renderings of the LXX and Vulgate[1] are consistent with this view, for they make a singular year of the hireling match precisely the singular year designated ἔτι ἐνιαυτὸς ὡς ἐνιαυτὸς μισθωτοῦ/ *Adhuc in uno anno quasi anno mercenarii.*

If the argument of Duhm and Marti fails at this point, then there is no force in an appeal to the parallel in Isa. xvi 14. Indeed, it is equally possible that the reading שלוש שנים of 1QIs[a] arises from an attempt to harmonize the two texts.[2]

כבוד · כבוד קדר may denote either Kedar's (military) dominance (cf. with D.K. viii 7, x 18, xvi 14, xvii 3f), or its illustrious leaders (so Saadya, אגלא); either interpretation could be predicated of the verb כלה.[3]

קדר. The word denotes a particular Arabian tribe in Gen. xxv 13 but is used elsewhere,[4] as here, of all the desert people east and south of Palestine.[5]

שאר מספר קשת. The versions all follow the M.T. in understanding שאר as a noun in the construct which is predicated of the verb ימעטו. For the LXX and Vulgate גבורי בני קדר is an absolute following שאר מספר קשת[6] but for the Targum and Peshitta the phrase is understood to be in apposition to גבורי בני קדר and a second subject of the verb ימעטו.

The word ושאר is read by Saadya as a waw consecutive with perfect and he renders the initial phrases: 'There will remain (ויבקי) a small number of their archers and their heroes will decrease...'[7] In his notes he observes that מספר is capable of the meaning 'small number' and for this usage he compares

---

1 The Peshitta follows the M.T. more closely and the Targum – 'at the end of the years' – is no help.

2 Cf. Wildberger. That no reading שנים (as opposed to שנה) is attested further weakens the case for adopting the reading of 1QIs[a]. Here the old maxim *difficilior lectio potior* is appropriate.

3 For a personal subject of כלה, cf. Isa. i 28, xxix 20, xxxi 3; for an abstract subject, cf. xvi 4.

4 Cf. with Gray Isa. xlii 11, lx 7; Jer. ii 10.

5 So Rosenmüller. Saadya appears to take this view: he notes that the oracle opens with a rebuke against the Dedanites but closes with notice of the punishment of the Sons of Kedar, 'for the many Arabian tribes all had dealings with each other and were as one people'.

6 I.e. שאר is followed by five genitives (so Delitzsch, who compares Isa. x 12).

7 So, apparently independently, Eitan. N.E.B. adopts this view.

Gen. xxxiv 30 (ואני מתי מספר 'My numbers are few' – N.E.B.)
and Jer. xliv 28. The interpretation has the merit that it makes
two parallel clauses of the verse, and avoids understanding the
verse as composed of five consecutive constructs.

Lowth (so Cheyne and Marti), referring to the Vulgate's
sagittariorum fortium, proposes to read גִּבֹּרֵי קֶשֶׁת 'mighty bowmen' for the M.T.'s קֶשֶׁת גבורי. This conjectural restoration is
probably occasioned[1] by the view that קֶשֶׁת properly denotes
'bows' rather than 'bowmen'. A similar view of קֶשֶׁת is taken by
Kissane who proposes the emendation רומי קשת after the phrase
רומה קשת 'bowmen' in Jer. iv 29.

On the other hand, the Vulgate, Peshitta and Saadya trans-
late the word קֶשֶׁת 'archers' (Vulg.: *sagittariorum*, Pesh.: *qšt*,
Saadya: רמאתהם) and with Rosenmüller we may suppose that
the word קֶשֶׁת 'bow' can by metonymy indicate 'bowmen'
collectively.[2]

That the Arabs were noted as bowmen is clear from Gen. xxi
20 where Ishmael is recorded as having appropriated the art (so
Rashi). According to Qimhi the prophecy against the sons of
Kedar was occasioned because of their oppressive behaviour
towards Israel at the time, perhaps that they attacked Israel as
allies of the king of Assyria.

The concluding authentication of the prophecy as a word of
Yahweh, the God of Israel, matches the similar conclusion of
verses 1–10. No important textual or exegetical questions are
raised by the words.

---

1 Lowth himself offers no explanation other than that his emendation 'seems
right'.
2 Hitzig, who compares 1 Kings xix 18 where 'knees' (ברכים) stands for the number of individual men.

2

Exegesis and Historical Background

Verses 1–10

As has been indicated in the textual commentary above, the rabbinic commentators ibn Janah, ibn Ezra and Rashi regard this prophecy in the light of Daniel v, and by reference to that text they interpret a number of the words and phrases of Isa. xxi 1–10. For these authorities, therefore, the prophecy as a whole concerns the fall of Belshazzar and the Babylonian empire at the hands of Darius the Mede. However, the legendary character of the book of Daniel together with the second-century date to which it is generally ascribed render such a comparison with the detailed deductions drawn from it highly questionable. It remains of value, however, as an indication that Jewish tradition from comparatively early times considered that the prophecy concerned the fall of the Neo-Babylonian empire, which we know to have taken place at the hands of Cyrus II of Persia in 539 B.C.[1]

In general, this view of the prophecy is adopted by subsequent commentators. Thus, for example, Rosenmüller (1793) states that the prophecy was obviously delivered at the same time as that of Isa. xiii and concerns (see verse 9) the fall of Babylon at the hands of Cyrus. The contents of the prophecy, to the smallest detail, match exactly the accounts of that fall preserved in other ancient authors. It is for Rosenmüller beyond question that the poet (not, of course, Isaiah) was himself present in Babylon and witnessed in person the events that he describes.

The ancient authors to whom Rosenmüller refers are the Greek historians Herodotus and Xenophon.[2] In their accounts of the fall of Babylon at the hands of Cyrus both authors recount that the Babylonians in the centre of the city were dancing and making merry at a festival (Herodotus) which lasted all

---

1 See *C.A.H.*, III, p. 224.
2 See *Histories* I 191 and *Cyropaedia* VII 15.

63

night long (Xenophon) and consequently were ill-prepared to defend the city. These accounts together with the story of Belshazzar in Daniel v are held by Rosenmüller to match precisely the scene of the feasting princes depicted in Isa. xxi 5 as well as the reference in verse 4 to the evening of pleasure (נשף חשקי) which was turned to trembling. Further correspondence of details is seen by him in the reference to asses and camels in verse 7, for Xenophon mentions the important part played by camels in Cyrus's defeat of Croesus (*Cyropaedia* VII 27), and Herodotus that played by asses in Darius Hystaspis's battles against the Scythian horsemen.[1] For Rosenmüller, therefore, Isa. xxi 1–10 reflects accurately the military characteristics of the Persian armies.

Rosenmüller's understanding of the historical background of the prophecy may be regarded as the orthodox critical view of the matter. It is followed, for example, by Delitzsch (1), though he initially differed from Rosenmüller in considering that there was nothing inherently improbable in Isaiah's having composed it.[2] In his treatment of Isa. xiii, which he also initially attributed to Isaiah, he concluded that Isaiah had clearly perceived the pattern of Yahweh's activity in history and seen that the overthrow of the Babylonian empire would follow *proteron–hysteron* the overthrow of the Assyrian. 'The fact that so far-reaching an insight was granted to him into the counsels of God, was not merely founded on his own personality, but rested chiefly on the position which he occupied in the midst of the first beginnings of the age of the great empires.'[3] More particularly Isa. xxxix indicates that in Hezekiah's time Isaiah had seen that ultimate judgement would be inflicted by the Babylonian empire rather than by the Assyrian. These earlier comments of Delitzsch are of considerable importance in regard to the transmission of the text of Isa. xxi and to them we shall have occasion to return.

P. Kleinert was the first to question what I have described as critical orthodoxy. In fact Kleinert was anticipated by

1 *Histories* IV 129; according to Rosenmüller, the asses were probably ridden by (Persian) Carmanians.
2 In the 4th edn of his commentary Delitzsch adopts the orthodox critical view, having explicitly changed his mind; for his comments, see 4th edn, *ad loc.*
3 E.T. (Martin), p. 296.

G. Smith,[1] but the latter scholar did not provide a critical and exegetical justification for his suggestion. To him the language of the prophecy, its terseness, its weighty expression and its formative power[2] tell decisively against a date in the sixth-century Babylonian period. Such characteristics distinguish it very markedly from the allegedly comparable Isa. xiii f and xxxiv, as well as from the Babylonian oracles of Jeremiah and Ezekiel.

Those prophecies from the book of Isaiah which concern the downfall of Babylon in the sixth century B.C. (Isa. xiii f and xlv ff) depict that event as an occasion of comfort and joy for Judah, which had hitherto experienced the overpowering might of her tyranny. Isa. xxi, on the other hand, offers a message (including the phrase 'Babylon is fallen', verse 9) which, so far from being an occasion of triumph and relief, is one of terror and anguish (see verses 3f) for God's people, for whom 'as threshed' (verse 10) the prophet feels painful and resigned sympathy. Finally, while the Medes (verse 2) were known as destroyers of Babylon in the sixth century (cf. xiii 17; Jer. li 11, 28), the Elamites (verse 2) were not. It was the Aryan Persians, not the Semitic Elamites to whom hopes for freedom from Babylon were directed. Elamites are indeed mentioned by prophetic writers of the time but simply as one of the peoples who, like Assyria, were to be brought low before Nebucha-drezzar's onslaught (Jer. xlix 34ff, Ezek. xxxii 24).

For Kleinert such difficulties prompt the question whether a fall of Babylon in Isaiah's own time might not fit better the language and expression of the prophecy. Because the prophecy follows immediately that of chapter xx, and because chapter xx concerns Sargon's capture of Ashdod in 711 B.C., he posits that Assyrian king's capture of Babylon in 710 (*C.A.H.*, III, p. 50) as the true background to Isa. xxi 1–10. Kleinert finds confirmation of his hypothesis in a number of references in the prophecy. First, verse 2 designates the attacker as *bôgēd* and *šôdēd*; the retrospective notice of Isa. xxxiii 1, 'Woe to thee that spoilest, and thou wast not spoiled (*šdd*); and dealest treacherously and they dealt not treacherously (*bgd*) with thee', clearly indicates

---

1 In *Transactions of the Society of Biblical Archaeology* (London, 1873), p. 329.
2 All of it is in vocabulary and thought demonstrably comparable to other Isaianic material.

the Assyrians. Secondly, the reference to Elamites and Medes (verse 2) as attackers may be understood in the light of the fact that Sargon conquered Elam in 721 and Media in 715. Isa. xi 11 and 2 Kings xvii 6, xviii 11 mention Elam and Media as places to which exiles from the Northern Kingdom were transported, and Isa. xxii 6 suggests that Elamites served as loyal vassals in the Assyrian army. Thirdly, the caravan of asses and camels indicates not a campaign march, but a column of booty wagons conducted by cavalry; mention of such columns is typical of Assyrian records of the time. As an example Kleinert quotes Sennacherib's description (Bellino cylinder; cf. Luckenbill, II, no. 270) of his spoils following the battle of Kish (702 B.C.): 'The chariots, wagons, horses, mules, asses, camels and (Bactrian) camels which (the enemy) had forsaken at the onset of battle, my hands seized.'

Kleinert's second main point is that the fall of Babylon at the hands of Sargon was one in which Judah and its prophet must have had a burning interest. The sickness and recovery of Hezekiah, which Kleinert dates in 712, afforded Merodach-baladan of Babylon an occasion to send an embassy to Jerusalem with the purpose of seeking an alliance with Hezekiah against the common Assyrian foe (2 Kings xx). Hezekiah's enthusiastic treatment of that embassy suggests that Judah was inclined to see in Babylon and Merodach-baladan a hope of deliverance; to Isaiah, however, the terrible truth was revealed that Babylon would fall, that Judah would continue on the threshing-floor (verse 10) and that night would continue to darken Edom (verses 11f). The prophecy, following that of chapter xx (711 B.C.), is to be dated in 710 when the decreed fate of Babylon was set in motion.

Kleinert's treatment of the prophecy was substantially accepted by T. K. Cheyne in his *Prophecies of Isaiah* first published in 1880. Cheyne noted, however, that the evidence in favour of Kleinert's dating was largely exegetical and that as such it would not command universal assent. He further gladly admitted that 'a fuller knowledge of the circumstances of the Jews might conceivably enable us to reconcile the prophecy with a date at the close of the exile'.

By 1895, in his publication *Introduction to the Book of Isaiah*, Cheyne had changed his mind, and he then advanced a number of exegetical considerations to meet the more important points raised by Kleinert.[1] It is clear that to a considerable extent Cheyne was influenced in his change of heart by the arguments advanced against Kleinert and in favour of the 'orthodox' view in two important commentaries published in Germany in the intervening years, viz. that of C. F. A. Dillmann (1890) and that of B. Duhm (1892).

For Dillmann the fatal objection to Kleinert's understanding of the prophecy was the fact that Elam and Media, represented in the prophecy as attacking Babylon (verse 2), were enemies of Sargon and indeed were allied with Babylon against him.[2] Furthermore, it is most unlikely that Isaiah with his indefatigable dislike of all alliances would have regarded with grief and dismay the (even enforced) ending of an alliance with Babylon. On the contrary, the prophet is depicted (verse 8) as long awaiting with anticipation the fall of Babylon together with its gods.

While he is prepared to agree with Kleinert that some of the language of the prophecy is Isaianic, Dillmann is concerned to point out that some of it is not. Apart from individual words and phrases,[3] Dillmann suggests that the general lack of clarity (verses 2, 4, 7, 9), the emphasis on personal feelings (verse 3) and the distinction between prophet and watchman (verse 6) tell against Isaianic authorship. On the contrary, they suggest an exilic prophet who awaited long and anxiously Babylon's end and who, being unknown to his contemporaries, properly described himself as a watchman. He concludes that the prophecy is to be dated just before Cyrus's campaign of 539 B.C. which ended in Babylon's fall and is as old as that of Isaiah xiii but from a different hand.

Dillmann and Duhm both comment further on the mention in verse 2 of Elam and Media. For them it is significant that Cyrus, before he conquered the Medes in 550–549, and constituted their district part of his empire, was king of Anshan, a place which, with its capital Susa, so far from being Persian,

---

1 It is not necessary to enter into the details of Cheyne's somewhat agonized reappraisal of exegetical considerations.
2 In regard to xxii 6 Dillmann subscribes to the view that Elamite mercenaries served in Sennacherib's army.
3 For which, see Dillmann, *ad loc.*

was situated in the eastern or northern district of Elam.[1] It is consequently reasonable to suppose that from the Babylonian point of view Cyrus's armies should be designated Elamites and Medes.

These criticisms of Kleinert's views (particularly in regard to his treatment of Elam and Media), together with Dillmann's argument that Elamites and Medes (verse 2) denote the united forces of Cyrus, are reproduced in the majority of later commentators[2] who are thereby prompted to champion anew the orthodox critical view of the prophecy. It is convenient here to record that Galling, who accepts this view, attempts to define more precisely the date of the prophecy on the basis of our increased knowledge of the movements of the last Babylonian king, Nabonidus, derived from the newly discovered Harran inscriptions.[3] For Galling, 539 (the date of Babylon's fall) is the *terminus ad quem* of the prophecy, which can be no *vaticinium ex eventu*, as Cyrus did not destroy the images of the Babylonian gods (cf. verse 9) but rather was concerned to foster the cults of his subject peoples. The conquest and annexation of Media is, in the light of verse 2, the initial *terminus a quo*. This can, however, be brought down to 546, the date of Nabonidus's return to Babylon from his sojourn in the Arabian desert. For the fact that Isa. xxi 11f and 13ff are concerned with upheaval in the deserts to the south of Palestine answers to what is likely to have been the situation there after Nabonidus returned to Babylon.[4] That these oracles are closely connected with Isa. xxi 1–10 (even if they were added by a redactor), suggests that all three oracles were concerned with the same political situation. The situation involved on the one hand unrest amongst the Arab tribes following Nabonidus's departure and on the other hand the united Persian empire being then in a position to mount a pincer attack on Babylon, the Medes attacking from the north, the Elamites from the south. Such a situation would

---

1 See, with Dillmann, particularly Halévy in *R.E.J.* (1889), 162ff.

2 So e.g. Cheyne (*I.B.I.*), Marti, Gray, Procksch, Fohrer, Kaiser, Galling and Wildberger. Kaiser and Galling follow *C.A.H.*, iv, in giving 553 B.C. as the date for Cyrus's defeat and annexation of the Medes. Wildberger argues that the use of the term 'Medes' in xiii 17 and of 'Medes and Elamites' in xxi 2 may suggest that the prophecies were compiled before Cyrus the Persian gained complete mastery of these peoples; see further below.

3 For which, see Gadd.

4 For details, see on these prophecies below.

be fraught with anxiety and uncertainty for the Jews and yet it would fill them with hope that their time of exile was nearly at an end. In short, the situation was similar to that nearly two centuries earlier when the words of Isaiah were proclaimed in the tension-filled time of the Syro–Ephraimite war (Isa. vii).

Galling's account of this prophecy cannot be evaluated without reference to the plausibility of his treatment of the other prophecies of the chapter on which substantially it is dependent. It is nonetheless based, as are others of the orthodox critical school, upon a particular interpretation of the all-important reference to Elam and Media in verse 2, viz. that it contains a reference to the united forces of Cyrus.

In 1898, W. H. Cobb published another attempt to attribute the prophecy to the eighth century B.C. and to the hand of Isaiah of Jerusalem. Cobb believed that Jerusalem rather than Babylon was the beleaguered city of verses 1–8, and that consequently the prophet's distress is of the same sort as that portrayed in chapter xxii 1–14. Verse 9 refers to a different situation, namely, the fall of the Assyrian empire, for which the name Babylon is used. For Cobb the similarity of words and expressions in chapters xxi 2–7 and xxii 4–7, 12–14 is so striking that when placed side by side they amount almost to 'a continuous narration'. For example, the enemies of verse 2 (the Elamites and Medes) are matched by the enemies of xxii 6 (Elam and Kir). The eating and drinking of the princes (verse 5) is matched in xxii 12 by the feasting of the inhabitants of Jerusalem. Such similarities indicate for Cobb that xxi 1–8, like xxii 1–14, is concerned with the Assyrian pressure on Jerusalem at the end of the eighth century B.C. (705–700) and the reference to Elam in verse 2, like that of xxii 6, indicates that Elamites were serving in Sennacherib's army.

In verse 9 Cobb argues that Babylon stands for the united world power Assyria–Babylon which, with its gods, is itself to fall when Yahweh's purposes for Jerusalem are fulfilled. 'As the representative city of Jahve is now threatened by heathen Asshur, so the representative city of that kingdom shall then be destroyed.' But in order that his dating of the prophecy should not be entirely dependent upon the identification of Babylon with Assyria, Cobb proposes another possibility for verse 9, viz. that it concerns Sennacherib's capture of Babylon in 704 (cf. *C.A.H.*, III, pp. 63f), which the prophet sees as the only possible outcome of an attempt by Hezekiah to enlist the support of Merodach-baladan. Such an attempt on the part of Hezekiah is assumed by Cobb as natural in view of his having sent an embassy to Egypt (Isa. xxx 6). Cobb sees in Isa. xxi 7 and 9 references to the dispatch of presents in a guarded convoy to Merodach-baladan in Babylon (verse 7) and, after a period of suspense, its return (verse 9) with the accompanying revelation that Babylon is fallen and therewith Judah's hopes for freedom.

Cobb's views have attracted little or no support, and with justice they are described by Marti as 'geistreich'. Apart from the fact that the unity of thought in the prophecy is quite destroyed and the text reduced to a number of somewhat unrelated sections, his arguments are tortuous and poorly based. For example, while his comparison of chapters xxi and xxii indicates some points of contact, it obscures many of the differences by the dubious device of suggesting that the verses, juxtaposed, form a continuous narration. Secondly, his argument that Babylon stands for Assyria is based largely upon observations of C. P. Tiele[1] who, justifying the title of his work, was concerned to show with a wide perspective the essential unity of the history of these two nations. To appropriate such observations for the purpose of supporting the allegation that Hebrew authors did not always distinguish the two powers is little short of absurd.

In 1900 and 1913 two British scholars, W. E. Barnes and C. Boutflower, both published articles urging that Isa. xxi 1–10 be attributed to Isaiah and dated in Assyrian times.

Barnes urges that the exegetical difficulties presented by the oracle are fewer and less important on the assumption that it belongs to the reign of Hezekiah than on the assumption that it belongs to the time of Cyrus's capture of Babylon in 539. Amongst the difficulties he adduces for the orthodox critical view are, e.g.: (verse 2) Cyrus never styled himself an Elamite, nor was he known as such either in the bible or in Persian monuments; (verses 3f) the distress of the prophet at the fall of Babylon alluded to in verse 2 is very difficult to understand

---

1 *Babylonische–assyrische Geschichte* (8 vols., Gotha, 1886–8).

if it marks the end of the exile and, in any case, is at odds with the apparent satisfaction of verse 9; (verse 5) while it matches the 'scandalous' accounts of Herodotus and Xenophon, it does not match the Nabonidus–Cyrus Chronicle (cf. *A.N.E.T.*, pp. 314ff) which states that Cyrus entered Babylon without fighting; the latter notice is usually regarded as more reliable than the former.

Barnes himself assumes that verses 1–5 concern not Babylon, but Jerusalem threatened from the south-west (the area of the Egyptian border) by Sargon II's forces (including Elamite and Median auxiliaries). In this situation the Judaeans mistakenly put their hopes in and rejoice over (verse 5; cf. xxii 13) an alliance with Merodach-baladan, *de facto* king of Babylon. In this connexion verses 6–9 contain Isaiah's prophecy of Merodach-baladan's fall and the end of Babylon in 710. Among the advantages of such a view Barnes notes that the prophet's display of lively distress (verses 3f) is better explained if the object of the threat (verse 2) is Jerusalem rather than Babylon. That he displays (if not satisfaction) cold impartiality at the fall of Babylon (verse 9) is also better explained on the assumption that Babylon is an ally of Judah – one more broken reed upon which the people were tempted to lean. With this assumption the sympathetic tone of verse 10 (Israel as crushed) is in accord.

Barnes's account of the prophecy has much to commend it. His criticisms of the orthodox critical view are well directed and telling, and his explanation of the reactions of the prophet far less strained. His exegetical arguments (and such primarily they are) constitute what is (necessarily) a somewhat speculative hypothesis, but it is a hypothesis that meets the major problems confronting exegetes. On the other hand, the very fact that he is able to lay all such problems on the basis of a hypothesis for parts of which (at least) there is no support from tradition[1] itself suggests some doubts about its correctness. Further, it should be noted that one part of Barnes's hypothesis rests upon ready and uncritical acceptance of the view that the Elamites and Medes of verse 2 (cf. xxii 6) were auxiliaries in the Assyrian army.

Boutflower's account of the oracle is not dissimilar to that of

---

[1] E.g. his supposition that verses 1–5 concern a threat to Jerusalem from the south-west.

Barnes, though there are some important differences. For Boutflower, the views of Smith and Kleinert were substantially correct but they were wrong to suggest that the fall of Babylon mentioned was that of 710. For Sargon, like Cyrus, entered the city peacefully and, so far from according its gods sacrilegious treatment (see verse 9), he outdid his predecessors in the costly offerings that he made at their shrines (see Luckenbill, II, no. 184). If then Cyrus's capture of Babylon cannot be the point of the oracle, neither can Sargon's. Boutflower solves this problem by supposing that verses 1–5 (verse 2b excepted) refer to Sargon's Babylonian campaign of 710 while verses 6–10 constitute a prophecy of the destruction of Babylon and its gods by Sennacherib in 689. With this latter view of verses 6–10 Sennacherib's Bavian inscription (cf. Luckenbill, II, no. 340) is in agreement: 'The gods dwelling therein . . . my men took and they broke them in pieces.' Boutflower regards it as significant that the Assyrian word used for 'broke them in pieces' (*ushabbiruma*) is 'radically identical to the שבר of verse 9' (cf. Erlandsson, apparently independently).

For Boutflower, the all-important half verse 'Go up, Elam . . .' is the voice of God and it is parenthetical. The prophet is afforded *en passant* a vision of the fall of Assyria, the devastator of Babylon. Again the prophecy was an accurate one, and Boutflower expends considerable effort to show that it was exactly fulfilled in the circumstances of the fall of Nineveh in 612 B.C. Thus, it was Cyaxares at the head of a Median army who dealt the final blow to Nineveh (see Herodotus, *Histories* I 106). Secondly, Boutflower recalls that Nineveh was threatened by a 'very great multitude of barbarians . . . (that) had come against (the king of Assyria) from the sea'.[1] In all probability it is the Elamites attacking Assyria from the Persian Gulf who are described in this report. Nabonidus's notice (see *A.N.E.T.*, pp. 308f) concerning the fall of Nineveh is cited by Boutflower as evidence to suggest that, while the Median forces actually captured Nineveh, Elamite and Babylonian forces were detained at Assyria's southern border.[2] Thus

---

1 So, according to Boutflower, Abydenus (a disciple of Berosus).
2 No reference is in fact made to the southern border of Assyria in this text, which states that the Babylonian Nabopolassar declined to take part in the destruction of Assyrian temples.

Isaiah's prophecy was exactly fulfilled. 'Go up, Elam . . .' –
Elam is to lead the way (by attacking Assyria from the sea);
'besiege, O Media' – Cyaxares the Median was to carry out the
siege and capture of Nineveh.

Boutflower's treatment of the oracle is consistent with what he
says of it: 'No prophecy was ever better interpreted by its
fulfilment.' His view that Isaiah initially spoke (verse 1–5) of a
campaign against Babylon by Sargon in 710 and then waited
until approximately 689 to announce its fulfilment (verses 6–10)
is just conceivable; indeed it is even possible to agree that it is
consistent with a 'long' (Boutflower's interpretation) wait by
Isaiah on his watchtower; but that Isaiah *en passant* should
have been vouchsafed a vision (correct to the smallest degree)
of an event (viz. the fall of Nineveh) which took place a hundred
years later is not consistent with what we know of prophecy
nor is it *a priori* likely. Further, in order to make a case for his
view, Boutflower is obliged to make a number of historical
assumptions for which he has little or no evidence. Boutflower's
treatment of the oracle is thus implausible, and implausible
simply because he insists on finding for every phrase of it a
detailed historical fulfilment over a period of at least one
hundred years.

Amongst more recent commentators on Isaiah, the interpretation of the prophecy offered by E. J. Kissane (1960) agrees in
part with that of Cobb (and it is apparently independent of it).
For Kissane the orthodox critical view is open to question on a
number of grounds; for example, the prophet speaks from the
standpoint of Palestine rather than from that of Babylonia, and
his emotion (verses 3 ff) is quite inexplicable if Babylon alone
is to fall. The apparently contradictory data of the text can be
reconciled by taking verses 1–2 to refer to the oppression of
Israel, the end of the prophecy (as it stands) to the fall of
Babylon at the hands of Cyrus, and the intervening verses to the
long period of waiting for the end of oppression. For Kissane,
however, the prophecy, like that of Isa. xiii, may originally
have concerned not the oppression and subsequent fall of
Babylon, but that of Assyria or its capital Nineveh. The
substitution of Babylon for the original reference probably took
place during the exile, thereby giving further significance and
point to the original prophecy of Isaiah.

In support of his suggestion that Babylon was substituted for an original reference to Assyria, Kissane draws attention particularly to Isa. xxiii 13 where 'Assyria' has been supplanted by 'the land of the Chaldeans', and where a scribal note to this effect is incorporated in the text itself. He cites further 2 Chron. xxxiii 11 and Mic. iv 10 where 'Babylon' may have been added by a later hand.[1]

Kissane's detailed interpretation of Isa. xxi, being very similar to that of Cobb, is open to similar criticisms. Yet his more general theory that a prophecy of the eighth century B.C. may have been adapted in the period of the exile to the circumstances then obtaining is worthy of serious consideration as it is compatible with evidence derived from a comparison between certain of Jeremiah's (sixth-century) foreign oracles and certain of Isaiah's foreign oracles (see chapters 3 and 4 below).

A radically different view of Isa. xxi 1–10 is taken by the recent German commentator O. Kaiser (1973; E.T. 1974). For Kaiser, the poem is best seen on form-critical grounds as a late work of art composed by a devout Jew 'in the study or temple cell'. Such a view of the poem accounts for the alleged 'artificiality of its prophetic features, the transitions which can be observed in the use of traditional themes and its deliberate but by no means naïve dramatic construction'. For Kaiser, then, the poem is essentially a late apocalyptic work which portrays 'the imminent fall of the world city'. This fall is eschatological and with other 'woes of the final age' heralds the dawning of the age of salvation. The fabric of the oracle, then, is 'drawn from' the events leading up to the fall of Babylon in 539, and by reference to them the prophet portrays the eschatological scheme which he wished to reveal. For Kaiser such an understanding alone explains why the conclusion of the poem does not describe jubilation on the part of the prophet at the proclamation of liberation but rather consists of a 'compassionate address to Zion as a child constantly flayed on the threshing floor of history'.

Kaiser's assessment of Isa. xxi 1–10 is, on his own admission, based upon personal impressions. Moreover, it may be said to

---

1 See Kissane, p. 147.

lack precision. He gives no indication of the date of the activity of his 'Jew in the study or temple cell', and he does not compare the language and form of the verses of this oracle with those of the writings widely accepted as apocalyptic in Isa. xxiv–xxvii (commonly called the Isaiah Apocalypse). Such a comparison may be held to indicate that the prophetic features of Isa. xxi 1–10 are, by comparison with those of Isa. xxiv–xxvii, far from artificial. Indeed, the particular references in the former text (e.g. Elam, Media, Babylon) as well as the first-person account of the reception of visions and of their effect are radically different from the generalized and (certainly) artificial statements of the Isaiah Apocalypse. Further, no comparison of Isa. xxi 1–10 with other late apocalyptic writings (such as the book of Daniel) is drawn by Kaiser. The manifestly contrived style of such works with their future reference is entirely different from the vigorous and dramatic style of Isa. xxi 1–10 with its historical allusions and past reference.

If Kaiser is right in sensing a certain 'artificiality' in Isa. xxi 1–10, that artificiality, so far from being of a sort with that of admittedly apocalyptic writings, is capable of the general interpretation of the passage advanced by Kissane, viz. that the text has been reworked in order to make it relevant to a later situation. This explanation has the merit that it is consistent with the evidence furnished from a consideration of Jeremiah's foreign oracles (see below, chapters 3 and 4).

Verses 11 & 12

The rabbinic commentators, whether they incline to the view that verses 11–12 concern Edom or (Arabian) Dumah, do not appear to record specific traditions or opinions concerning the historical circumstances to which the oracle refers. It is true that ibn Janah characterizes Edom as an 'evil kingdom', but that is typical of the traditional Jewish attitude to Edom from 587 B.C. onwards. For by their gloating over and taking advantage of the downfall of Judah at the hands of the Babylonians, the Edomites earned the undying hatred of the Jews.[1] With this attitude the same commentator's explanation of Dumah is

---

1 Cf. Obadiah, Jer. xl 7ff and Ezek. xxv 12–14, Mal. i 2–5, Ps. cxxxvii 7 and Sir. l 25.

consistent, viz. that the evil kingdom of Edom is called 'Dumah'
by the prophet because they are a people '(justly) doomed to
(the silence of) destruction'.

By contrast, as a number of modern commentators have
observed, the oracle itself is apparently free from the marks of
hatred toward Edom characteristic of exilic and post-exilic
biblical references to that country. On the basis of this observation some are inclined to the view that the oracle cannot be
dated after 587.

Vitringa considers that the prophecy denotes a time of
calamity experienced by the Edomites in common with the
Jews. While the prophet is able to announce the dawn of relief
for Israel, he proclaims that the night of calamity is to continue
for Edom.[1] The time of this common calamity was for Vitringa
when Nebuchadrezzar invaded Palestine and took many
captives from Israel as well as from Edom and other Palestinian
peoples.[2]

Cheyne (*I.B.I.*),[3] apparently independently, adopts the same
point of view. Referring to the notices in Jeremiah (xxvii 3 and
xlix 7f, 28) which advert to the rebellion of Zedekiah together
with other Palestinian peoples against Babylon and to Babylon's
revenge upon Edom, he concludes that the Dumah oracle
belongs to 589, the date when Nebuchadrezzar moved into
Syria and sent detachments to deal with Palestine and its
neighbours. That Jeremiah's oracle against Edom (xlix) also
mentions Dedan suggests to Cheyne that Isa. xxi 13–15 may
also belong to this time. And with this comparatively late date
for the oracle, the 'Aramaic colouring' of Isa. xxi 11f is consistent.[4] But for Cheyne it is the equilibrium of feeling in the
prophet that constitutes the all-important indication that the
prophecy predates 587 (the year of the beginning of Judah's
hatred for Edom).

For other modern scholars the relationship of the oracle with
that of verses 1–10 provides a more important criterion for the

---

1 The motif 'Dawn for Israel, night for the gentiles' can be traced as far back as
the Targum and Palestinian Talmud (see ch. 1 above).
2 Vitringa does not indicate whether he has in mind the invasion of 597 B.C. or
that of 589–586.
3 In *P.I.* he dates the prophecy in Sargon's reign.
4 For Procksch's criticism of the argument, see below.

dating of it. Thus, for example, Marti[1] regards the two oracles as unmistakably from the same prophet because the question-and-answer form is common to both, as is the distinction between prophet and watchman; in both oracles the watchman's answer is indecisive; and the prophet's knowledge of the storms of the Negeb (verse 1) is consistent with his dwelling in a place to which the Edomites could readily be invited to return with further questions. Since, therefore, the oracle of verses 1–10 concerns the fall of Babylon at the hands of Cyrus in 539, the Dumah oracle must belong to the same period (i.e. between 549 and 538). The objection that the note of bitterness and hostility towards Edom is absent and that therefore the oracle must predate 586 is contested by Marti with the argument that the prophet merely displays in both oracles the same 'remarkable objectivity and neutrality'.[2]

Marti does not provide further indications for regarding the prophecy as belonging to the period 549–538. He is content to follow Duhm's similar supposition and to assert that the news of the fall of Babylon had prompted the Edomites to ask the prophet whether their own circumstances would now improve. For they were torn between the hope of freedom on the one hand and, on the other, fear of losing business interests with the demise of their trading partner Babylon. The prophet's answer is equivocal: just as in verses 1–10 he was unable to see clearly the results of the fall of Babylon for the Jewish people, so in the Dumah oracle the fate of Edom is regarded as uncertain. The morning of hope may appear to be dawning, but it is not certain that another night will not descend. In such circumstances the Edomites are encouraged to return at a later time to the prophet's dwelling place in southern Palestine for further information.

If Marti is inclined to regard the prophet's somewhat unsatisfactory answer to his enquiry as plausible, F. Buhl is not. For him it is not admissible that the prophecy should conclude with a note of unresolved ambiguity ('unaufgelösten Disharmonie') and consequently the words of the prophet's

---

1 Cf. the more recent presentation of such arguments by Wildberger, though for him Duma(t al Jandal), not Edom, is the burden of the prophecy.
2 The phrase is quoted from Duhm. Marti's arguments rather than Duhm's are discussed here because they are fuller.

answer must be taken to mean 'morning comes even though it is also night'. (For this translation, see the textual commentary above.) Buhl is of the opinion that the oracle indicates the period of Hezekiah's accession to the throne of Judah (shortly before 722 B.C. – *C.A.H.*, III, p. 388) when a movement towards emancipation from Assyria was developing among the vassal states of Palestine. Edom's king Kausmalak was among those who had paid tribute to Tiglath-pileser (745–728 B.C. – cf. *A.N.E.T.*, p. 282), and, with Philistia, Judah and Moab, she was involved shortly after 715 (*C.A.H.*, III, p. 388) in an abortive rebellion against Sargon, a rebellion which was crushed when Sargon invaded Ashdod and Gath in 712. The prophet's advice to the enquiring Edomites at an early stage in this period, viz. that they should remain in quiet anticipation of their freedom and that they should ask the prophet further about it at a later stage, is consistent with Isaiah's fundamental policy of caution. That Edom had a part in the abortive rebellion of 715–712, referred to above, indicates that the Edomites did not in fact follow the prophet's wise advice.[1]

Procksch is also of the opinion that the Dumah oracle belongs to this period (721–710 B.C.). The absence of hatred for Edom rules out a date in exilic or post-exilic times; and the fact that the oracle is parallel at some points to that concerning Moab in Isa. xv and xvi 1–5 serves to point to 715 when the Assyrian army subdued certain Arab tribes (cf. *C.A.H.*, III, p. 58, and Luckenbill, II, no. 17), arriving, so Procksch assumes, by way of Moab. Thus the Dumah oracle, like that concerning Moab, reveals one of Judah's neighbours turning to Jerusalem and receiving a prophetic message for the future (cf. Isa. xvi). Since Edom and Moab were close neighbours, it is reasonable to suppose that the circumstances reflected in both oracles are those of the same historical situation. On the assumption that Moab was subdued by the Assyrians as they advanced to impose tribute on the Arabian tribes, and further that Edom managed to avoid the same fate, it is entirely likely that Edomites enquired urgently of Jerusalem concerning their own future. For Procksch, the presence of Aramaisms in the oracle, so far from being evidence of a late date, is a further

---

1 For a similar view of the date of the prophecy, cf. Cheyne, *P.I.* In his later work (*I.B.I.*) Cheyne dates the oracle in the sixth century (see above).

indication of this period. For such dialectal forms are to be regarded as Edomite[1] or, more probably, as reflecting the international and business Aramaic known to have been employed at the time from e.g. Isa. xxxvi 11.

The arguments concerning the dating of the Dumah oracle which have so far been outlined may be said to turn upon one of two considerations, viz. either (*a*) the absence of anti-Edomite sentiment in the oracle or (*b*) the unity of the oracle with that preceding it. If the first consideration is adopted it follows that the period following *c.* 588 is excluded; if the second, the period immediately before the fall of Babylon in 539 may be positively indicated. Those further considerations which are advanced in order to suggest more precisely the date of the oracle (e.g. its dialectal colouring) are to an extent secondary and dependent upon the adoption of one of the foregoing.

Of the two considerations, (*a*) is the more likely, at least initially, to prove convincing. For while both considerations are to some extent the product of the personal impressions of the critic, it is easier to recognize the objectivity of the former than of the latter.[2]

A radically different approach to the Dumah oracle is that adopted by C. Rabin. In Rabin's opinion the language of the oracle is dialectal and reflects Isaiah's predilection for 'creating atmosphere' in a foreign oracle by making use of a word or words in the language of the nation concerned. The foreign phrase is not necessarily a correct expression in the relevant language but is coined as a 'stage' expression to indicate to the listener the particular nation and its language. As an illustration of what he has in mind Rabin cites the 'pseudo-Italianized English' of 'I no go' which can be readily understood by an Englishman but also suggests to him that the speaker is Italian. Secondly, the cryptic brevity and apparent triviality of the

---

1 This Procksch characterizes as close to 'Aramaic–Arabic'. More recently Edomite has been described by Naveh as a Canaanite dialect akin to Hebrew, Moabite and Ammonite. It is likely that as early as the sixth century B.C. the script employed in writing it was Aramaic (see Naveh, pp. 27f). Bartlett ('From Edomites to Nabateans') cites evidence for the use of the Aramaic language and script as far south as Teima from the period between the sixth and fourth centuries B.C.

2 For arguments against the unity of xxi 1–12, see Lohmann. He also considers that the 'objectivity and neutrality' of the Dumah oracle are more apparent than real.

Dumah oracle suggest to Rabin that it was an intricate piece of rhetoric which said much more than meets the eye and that, in the manner of Greek oracles, it revealed its meaning only after much pondering.[1]

Rabin considers that the language of the oracle reflects Arabic and that its real concern is with the Arabian oasis of Dumat al Jandal to which, he supposes, Edomites fled as refugees (cf. the similar flight in the Arabian oracle which follows). In their panic and trepidation they are pictured as having recourse to the oracle of Dumah, asking its god Wadd and his priests[2] what the future has in store for them. The prophecy as a whole is translated thus:

> Prophecy of Dumah. Someone from Seir calls out to me: 'Watchman/Shammarite, what watch of the night is it, watchman, what watch of the night is it?' The watchman/Shammarite replied: 'The morning has come, and the night is fulfilled. If ye have sinned/attacked, pray; if ye (truly) repent, ye will return home.'

Question and answer are ostensibly directed to and given by a city watchman, and, together with references to day and night, constitute a highly rhetorical formulation of the Edomites' concern. The question expresses their anxiety apparently in terms of the sleepless sufferer impatiently awaiting the morning watch. The answer 'If ye have sinned (or attacked), pray, etc.'[3] refers 'with all necessary clarity' to the attacks of Edom on Israel, or to the injustice and harm done by Edom to Israel and further indicates that these crimes are the reason for Edom's disaster.[4]

In his English article, Rabin makes no reference to the historical background of the oracle (as understood by him) other than by referring to Edom's crimes against Israel. The same reference to Edom's crimes reappears in his Hebrew article (p. 249) but here he makes further observations about

1 English, pp. 304f, 307.
2 Rabin considers that the use of the word שמר 'watchman' may be an allusion on Isaiah's part to the Arabian tribe of Shamar who (Rabin conjectures) may have originally inhabited Al-Jauf (English, pp. 305f; Hebrew, p. 247).
3 For a discussion of the linguistic and philological issues involved in this translation, see ch. 1 above.
4 So English, pp. 308ff.

the historical background of the oracle (pp. 250ff). First, he draws attention to Kaufmann's finding that in chapters i–xxxiii of Isaiah there is no trace of an attitude of vengeance or retribution against the nations, as there is, by contrast, in the chapters which follow chapter xxxiii. The positive doctrine of these earlier chapters is that repentance on the part of sinful nations will effect their forgiveness and this is clearly further exemplified in the Dumah oracle as Rabin understands it. Consequently, the oracle can be attributed to the early period of Isaiah.[1]

Secondly, Rabin observes that the Edomite refugees must have consulted the oracle of Dumah at a time when it was functioning normally as an important sanctuary. In this regard Rabin recalls Esarhaddon's notice (Luckenbill, II, nos. 318a, 536) that his father Sennacherib captured Dumah and brought its gods to Nineveh. In the same text Esarhaddon goes on to record that in answer to the request of Hazael, king of the Arabs, he restored the gods of the Arabs to their sanctuaries (probably in 676; see *C.A.H.*, III pp. 83ff). Since, then, Sennacherib silenced the oracle of Dumah, Rabin argues that the prophecy cannot be attributed to the years of his reign. Nor can the oracle belong to the time before Sennacherib, because that would require it to be dated before Isaiah's time (Hebrew, p. 250). Consequently Rabin concludes that the oracle belongs to the reign of Esarhaddon and of course to a period after he had restored the Arabian gods to their shrines (i.e. after 676; see *C.A.H.*, III, pp. 83ff). Rabin reaches this conclusion tentatively and with the explicit admission that Esarhaddon has left no record of an expedition to Edom (Hebrew, p. 251).

There are many points in Rabin's argument that are open to challenge – even on the assumption that his translation of the text is correct and that the prophecy refers to the shrine of Wadd at Dumat al Jandal. For example, why should not the prophet refer to Edomite refugees passing through Dumah in Sennacherib's time before he invaded the place? All that is required of the prophecy is that it should *depict* Edomite refugees as having recourse to the oracle of Dumah; a prophecy which (in Rabin's own words) is 'highly rhetorical' does not in the nature of the case have to be a *vaticinium ex eventu*, an accurate chronicle

---

[1] Hebrew, p. 250.

of precise historical events. And why, for that matter, is the time before Sennacherib excluded? Rabin suggests that it is impossible on the grounds that it is 'before the time of Isaiah' to whom, on the grounds adduced by Kaufmann, he is inclined to attribute the prophecy. But Isaianic oracles clearly predate the reign of Sennacherib (e.g. chapter xx explicitly mentions Sargon), and the year of Isaiah's call (Isaiah vi 1) is probably to be dated some thirty-five years before the accession of Sennacherib. Indeed such considerations render it very unlikely that Isaiah was active in Esarhaddon's reign (681–669 B.C.), as Rabin suggests; for then he would most probably have been over eighty years old. At any rate an oracle referring to events in Esarhaddon's reign is unlikely to belong, in Rabin's words, 'to the early period of Isaiah'.

Such matters, however, are trivial compared with one particular major discrepancy in Rabin's argument. How can an oracle whose purpose is (in Rabin's opinion) to invite Edomites to repent of their conspiracy against and attacks upon Israel be attributed 'to the early period of Isaiah', and, even tentatively, be dated in the time of Esarhaddon? If Rabin refers to Edomite treachery other than that of 590–586,[1] he does not make this plain; on the contrary, he appeals explicitly to the general biblical view that Edom incurred guilt by reason of her attacks upon and conspiracy against Israel (see Hebrew, p. 249).

If the recognition of this discrepancy occasions serious doubts about Rabin's historical observations, it has repercussions also for the author's philological arguments. Rabin suggests, for example, that בעה (first occurrence) has the sense 'to sin *or* attack' because such a meaning fits the context. But if the oracle does not contain a reference to Edomite treachery against Israel, the meanings 'sin' for בעה (first occurrence), 'pray' for בעה (second occurrence), and 'repent' for שוב find no place in it.

It is not here necessary to enter into the details of Rabin's interesting account of the history of the shrine at Dumat al Jandal. What does concern us is the question of the antecedent likelihood of an Israelite prophet (whether Isaiah or a later

---

[1] Such as, for example, that alluded to in 2 Chron. xxviii 17.

author) making use of an oracular answer of an obscure foreign deity in order to convey to Israel the word of Yahweh concerning Edom. The question is equally pertinent whether the prophet's allusion to that oracle relates to an historical situation known to him or whether it arises solely from his prophetic imagination. The answer to the question must surely be that it is unlikely in the extreme. For no instance even remotely comparable can be cited from the prophetic literature of the O.T. And it is not surprising that none is in fact cited by Rabin.

What may be characterized as a form-critical account of the Dumah oracle is given by P. Lohmann and by means of this approach he posits a date for the oracle at a time towards the end of the exile.

Lohmann argues that the oracle should not be attributed to the author of verses 1–10. Indeed, so far from being properly an oracle, it is a secular poem which has later been adapted for use as a foreign oracle and, as such, it has been tacked on to the Babylonian oracle of verses 1–10. The poem underlying verses 11f is of a sort with the vintage songs alluded to in Isa. xvi 10 and Jer. xxv 30 and with the harlot's song quoted in Isa. xxiii 16. The watchman's song constitutes a joke ('Scherzliedchen') current in the ancient Near East and known to the prophet and his hearers. The song may, indeed, be very old and, as is the case with the Song of Songs, its Aramaisms need not tell against this view. Such poems are by their very nature anonymous and timeless.

Lohmann conjectures that, in its original form, the song began with the word בָּעֶרֶב which was subsequently displaced and wrongly affixed to the beginning of verse 13.[1] Lohmann further conjectures that מִשַּׁעַר ('from the gates') stood where now משעיר ('from Seir') is read. The term שמר denotes a city watchman[2] who is questioned by those waiting impatiently outside the city gates as to how late in the night it is and how long there is to wait until dawn and the opening of the gates. The joke is occasioned by the mischievous and short-tempered

---

1 He notes that the LXX at verse 13 does not have a word corresponding to the M.T.'s בערב and he further observes that the word בערב in the M.T. is superfluous.

2 Lohmann compares Song of Songs iii 3, Pss. cxxi 3 and cxxx 6.

reply of the watchman, who tells them in effect to go home and not to bother him further.[1]

The change from משער to משעיר was, however, no accident but was effected by the creative talent of a prophet. Thereby the poem became an oracle expressing hatred for the treacherous Edomites, and, when appended to Isa. xxi 1–10, was understood as a heathen oracle indicating that at the end of the exile day would dawn for Israel but night would descend upon Edom. What is intended by the last words of verse 12 (אם תבעיון etc.) within the heathen oracle is, to Lohmann, obscure and he is content to regard them simply as a survival of the original watchman's song.

To Lohmann it seems probable that the prophet who incorporated the watchman's song and made of it a foreign oracle was none other than the composer of verses 1–10. For both oracles are concerned with the same historical situation and they are juxtaposed in the literary tradition of Isaiah. In the Babylonian oracle there are expressed hatred and threat against Babylon and hope for the Jews; in the Edom oracle, threat and mockery are directed against Edom but hope is expressed for Judah. The difference of expression (e.g. the use of the unparalleled שמר 'watchman' for the prophet in verses 11, 12) can be accounted for by the recognition that verses 1–10 represent a prophetic composition but that verses 11f are a reworking of an existing secular composition.

Lohmann's treatment of the Dumah oracle has the considerable merit that it is able to give an account not merely of the meaning of the words of verses 11f but also of the form of the composition. His comparison with the use made of the harlot's song in Isa. xxiii 16 is particularly telling, and militates against Galling's particular criticisms of his views. For Galling asserts that it is antecedently improbable that a prophet should make use of such a drinking song to convey a message on so important a question as the dawning of salvation for Israel. Yet Galling appears to ignore the evidence of Isa. xxiii 16 where the harlot's song is used by the prophet to depict the fate of Tyre.

---

1 Lohmann is not inclined to decide between Buhl's translation of the reply ('morning comes while it is still night') and that of Duhm ('morning comes and also [i.e. at the same time] night'); whichever is adopted, the effect, for him, is the same.

Lohmann's account, moreover, has the merit that the 'allegorical' meaning which he detects (i.e. 'dawn for Israel, night for Edom') is consistent with the likely feelings of the Jews in exilic times, and, as has been mentioned above (p. 45), it is actually found in Jewish tradition as far back as the Targum and the Palestinian Talmud.

On the other hand, the rigidity of Lohmann's distinction between secular poem and prophetic oracle has been pressed further than is warranted by the evidence.[1] For example, his argument that the words must have been originally a secular poem because there is no explicit mention of divine inspiration is hardly convincing, for a number of heathen oracles lack such notices (see e.g. Isa. xvf). Again his insistence that שׁמר is not an O.T. designation for a prophet is not convincing; for, as has been observed above, to assert that שׁמר is not an O.T. designation for a prophet does not amount to grounds for denying that a prophet may have so described himself in a particular oracle. A further weakness of Lohmann's case lies in the fact that he is unable to give an account of the force of the last words of the oracle *qua* oracle; he has to content himself with giving a translation of the words appropriate to the poem's original situation: 'If you wish to ask, ask; go now and come back.' If he is unable to determine the sense of these words as part of the foreign oracle, his case for a distinction between secular song and foreign oracle is further weakened.

It is, however, the rigidity of Lohmann's distinction that enables him to find in verses 11f mockery of Edom and consequently to date the oracle (or adapted song) at a time after 587 and towards the end of the exile. But it may be urged equally well that the words of verses 11f are more simply (and therefore more plausibly) to be interpreted as a poetical expression of the prophet's teaching concerning Edom and that he has had recourse to the metaphor of the city watchman just as he has depicted his function in the previous oracle in terms of a look-out (מצפה). That the words of the oracle do not apparently give expression to anti-Edomite feeling remains *prima facie* an indication that the prophecy is pre-exilic.

Lohmann's further conclusion that the oracle is to be dated

---

1 His account (all-important to his theory) of the word משׁעיר rests purely upon conjecture.

in late exilic times because the prophet who adapted and made use of it is the author of verses 1–10 depends, of course, on his acceptance of the view that the latter prophecy is also to be dated in the same period. That, however, is not evident, and has not been conclusively demonstrated.

If for Lohmann form-critical methods illuminate the Dumah oracle, for K. Galling it is Babylonian historical records, and more specifically the recently published Harran inscriptions of the last Babylonian king, Nabonidus.[1] Noting that the Dumah oracle, like that which follows it, is concerned with the inhabitants of the deserts to the south-east of Judah he supposes that the whole of Isa. xxi reflects the historical situation following Nabonidus's return to Babylon after his campaign and subsequent ten-year sojourn in the oases of North Arabia. For Galling, Nabonidus's return to Babylon may be dated precisely in the years 546–545 B.C.[2]

There has been considerable discussion about the reasons for Nabonidus's protracted stay in North Arabia, but recent commentators favour the view that he went there on a military expedition with the ultimate intention of securing the trade route which ran along the eastern shore of the Red Sea.[3] Galling is content to recall, however, that Nabonidus himself mentions as the reason for his withdrawal from Babylon the avowed hostility of the great cities of Babylon and their hierarchies towards him and his religious policies.[4] At any rate, accompanied by his troops from 'Akkad and the Hatti-Land'[5] Nabonidus set forth 'on the road to Tema', Dadanu, Padakku ... and as far as Iatribu', subduing the oases of the Hijaz as far as Iatrib (Medina) and investing them with garrisons. At Teima he appears to have made his headquarters, building there a residence for himself and a shrine for his beloved god

1 For these texts, see Gadd.
2 The latter date is computed by excluding the king's year of accession. Gadd (p. 75) considers that it is not possible to be precise about the dates of the Arabian sojourn.
3 See S. Smith, *Isaiah*, pp. 38ff, quoted by Lindsay, p. 37; W. F. Albright in *B.A.S.O.R.* 82 (1941), pp. 11f, and Gadd, pp. 88f. For an earlier discussion, see R. P. Dougherty in *J.A.O.S.*, 1922, pp. 305ff.
4 Cf. Gadd, p. 88. For Nabonidus's actual words, see *ibid.* pp. 56ff.
5 The former term indicates native Babylonian troops; the latter, contingents from Syro-Palestine. Gadd supposes that in fact the Babylonian troops were sent back to Babylon under Belshazzar, while it was Syro-Palestinian troops (including Jews) who accompanied Nabonidus to Arabia (pp. 85ff).

Sin. Thereafter for ten years he moved from place to place, reviewing his garrisons, putting down rebellions on the part of the Arabs, and enjoying the benefits of 'wealth and abundance'. In regard to his suzerainty over particular Arab peoples, two recently discovered Thamudic inscriptions which mention 'the spear of the king of Babylon' and 'the War of Dedan', indicate 'the vivid impression made upon the inhabitants of the area already literate enough to record their recollections of so stirring an episode' (Gadd, p. 78). For Galling, mention of the War of Dedan may indicate either the original subjugation of that oasis, or the battles following a rebellion on its part.

It is, however, the triumphal return of Nabonidus to Babylon which is, in Galling's opinion, of such great importance to Isaiah xxi. Apparently, circumstances in Babylon in 545 were more favourable to Nabonidus and he was able to return to his capital and to resume work on his cherished plan of restoring the Sin temple at Harran. When he left Teima and as he travelled the desert road, he records that he received the homage of neighbouring kings (Gadd, p. 63). Yet, although the texts are naturally silent on the subject, Galling considers it reasonable to suppose that Nabonidus's departure must have raised in the hearts of the peoples of the west both turmoil and hope. While his departure did not necessarily entail the immediate decline of Babylonian dominance, it may have been thought to involve eventually substantial change for the area. Would the remaining Babylonian troops be able to contain the situation? Would all the various Arab tribes remain loyal? Would fighting break out among them? Such questions must have achieved new importance and significance as the king left the deserts of Arabia for his Babylonian homeland.[1]

Galling's understanding of Isa. xxi 1–10 has been considered above (pp. 68ff) and it is there shown to be essentially a variant of the orthodox critical view of the oracle. In Galling's opinion its concern is with the imminent fall of Babylon at the hands of the Persians – the Elamites and Medes of verse 2. Because, however, the oracle is followed by two prophecies[2] concerned *ex hypothesi* with the turbulence of desert peoples

---

1 Galling's views are tentatively accepted by Wildberger.
2 The theory is unaffected by the consideration that it was a redactor rather than a common author who combined the oracles.

south-east of Judah following Nabonidus's departure in 546/5, Galling believes it likely that verses 1–10 reflect the same situation and should therefore be dated between 545 and 540. As has been stated above, the orthodox critical view of the oracle stands or falls with the identification of Elam and Media in verse 2 with the united empire of Cyrus. In regard to Galling's particular further deduction, viz. that the oracle reflects the general disquiet in the west following Nabonidus's departure from Arabia, a particular question immediately presents itself: why does the oracle contain no mention of nor allusion to that departure of Nabonidus if it was the all-important cue to peoples of the west?

Where the Dumah oracle is concerned, Galling believes that the title 'Dumah' must refer to a specific place (as does e.g. Isa. xxii 1) and that that place is Dumat al Jandal in Arabia.[1] He further suspects that the reading of the minor Greek versions (for which see above) presupposes the original sense: 'summon (or someone is summoning)[2] to me those who have fled from Seir'. Just as following 545 Dedanites found shelter in the oasis of Teima (verses 13ff), so here refugees from Dumah are pictured as fleeing via Seir to West Jordanian Edom and as having recourse to a Jewish prophet in order to ascertain their destiny. That they should do so is rendered less surprising by the further assumption that the refugees were in fact Jews, and that assumption in turn is rendered possible for Galling by the consideration that Jews are likely to have been amongst the soldiers and settlers introduced to the North Arabian oases by Nabonidus (see Gadd, pp. 85ff). At any rate, the likely tension arising after 545 between Babylonian troops and settlers on the one hand, and freedom-seeking Arabs on the other, may have furnished the occasion for such a flight of Jews from Dumah and for their anxious questioning of a Judaean prophet. His reply according to Galling could, in the circumstances, be nothing but enigmatic. The night of misery remained, but dawn would follow at some time in the future known only to Yahweh. Return for further questioning might find the prophet better able to furnish clearer answers.

1 He does not believe that the LXX's 'Edom' reflects a text preferable to the M.T.
2 Reading καλεῖ for κάλει.

Any account of so short and terse an oracle as the Dumah oracle must make assumptions. But the number of assumptions made by Galling are surely too numerous and tenuously based to command ready agreement. Above all, his exegesis of the oracle is substantially dependent upon his suggestion that the minor Greek versions indicate the true text and meaning of the oracle. It is very unlikely, however, that those versions bear witness to a Hebrew text divergent from the M.T. On the contrary, as has been argued above, their rendering bears all the marks of an attempt to clarify and elucidate the rendering of the LXX, with the wording of which it is substantially identical.

Another attempt to link the Dumah oracle with Nabonidus's Arabian campaign is that of J. Lindsay. He is not concerned to emend or alter the M.T., and he is content to reproduce without further comment the translation of the R.S.V. What is significant to him, however, is the word 'Dumah' in the title of the oracle, and the fact that it is 'in parallelism' with 'Seir'. The two words juxtaposed indicate that Edom is meant; and by Edom, Lindsay argues, the author seeks to depict a greater Edom, i.e. an area comprising both Edom itself and the area of its trade influence, extending as far east as Dumah and as far south-east as Dedan. That such a greater Edom was recognized by the Jews seems to be confirmed by such texts as Ezek. xxv 13 (which mentions Teman and Dedan as distant places in Edom against which Yahweh would stretch forth his hand). Similarly in Jer. xlix 7 Dedan is addressed by name within the context of an oracle addressed to Edom.

That Nabonidus's Arabian campaign of 552 affected Edom as well as the Arabian oases themselves may be inferred from the Nabonidus Chronicle (*A.N.E.T.*, p. 305) which states that in the course of the campaign it was necessary to reduce a certain city whose name ends in '*dummu*'; this is now generally taken to denote Edom rather than Dumah.[1] For Lindsay, then, the evidence of the Babylonian texts concerning Nabonidus's itinerary and campaign reflect, as do the biblical texts cited

---

1 See S. Smith against W. F. Albright in *J.R.A.S.*, 1925, pp. 293ff, 508ff; A. K. Grayson, *Assyrian and Babylonian Chronicles* (New York, 1975), p. 282; W. G. Lambert in *Proceedings of the 5th Seminar for Arabian Studies, Oxford 1971* (London, 1972), p. 55.

above, the reality of a greater Edom. This, he submits, is the subject of the oracle of Isaiah xxi 11f.

While the historical and geographical considerations advanced by Lindsay seem to be unexceptionable, his treatment of the Dumah oracle is far from satisfactory. On the one hand he accepts Lehman's view (for which, see p. 39 n. 2 above) that the original reading of the text of the title was 'Edom' and not 'Dumah'. On the other, the drift of his argument requires that the oracle contain in parallelism (his word) Seir and Dumah (not Edom); for in that way, rather as the Edom oracle of Jer. xlix makes mention of Dedan, Isaiah's oracle can be held to reflect the greater Edom whose probable existence is attested on other grounds. But either 'Edom' or 'Dumah' was the original reading of the title. Lindsay must decide; he cannot have it both ways.

Similar inconsistency in Lindsay's argument may be detected in his assertion that Lehman's finding (viz. that 'Edom' was the original reading of the title) 'reinforces the opinion long held by a majority of scholars that the M.T. reflects the close association in the minds of Isaiah's contemporaries between Edom and Dumah'. It is hard to see how this could be the case if Dumah were not in fact mentioned either in the oracle or its title. Furthermore, if the oracle refers to Nabonidus's overthrow of Adummu/Edom, as Lindsay suggests, it is hard to see how the M.T. can be held to reflect any association whatsoever in the minds of *Isaiah's* contemporaries.[1]

Kaiser's view of the Dumah oracle, though expressed very tentatively, is of a sort with his view of the oracle of verses 1–10 and merits similar criticisms. He supposes that the poem, originally without title and introductory words ('One is calling to me from Seir'), was appended to verses 1–10 as a word of comfort to the faithful concerning the dawn of salvation following the fall of the world capital (verse 9); 'Morning is coming though it is still night.' This view, he says, is 'the least artificial because it avoids all speculation as to why a prophet or writer of Judah should suddenly be interrogated by Edomites or be concerned with what happens to them'. It is difficult to be sure what Kaiser means by his phrase 'least artificial' ('ungekün-

---

1 If by the use of the name Isaiah he means to suggest the later author of this oracle, he does not make his intention clear.

steltste'). It seems to me, however, that his own treatment is in fact very highly artificial and that one aspect of that artificiality is to be seen in his arbitrary and speculative deletion of the introductory words of the oracle.

Kaiser's alternative suggestion that the oracle is a late redactional addition made in order to complete a full complement of foreign oracles seems to rest ultimately upon the view that its Aramaisms indicate at least an exilic (and probably a post-exilic) date. Procksch's observations on the early use of Aramaic have been noted above and in the light of them we may discount the most important element in Kaiser's argument. What remains is purely speculative.

Further observations about the historical background to the Dumah oracle are made in connexion with the Arabian oracle; see below.

Verses 13–15

Apart from the Talmudic tradition[1] (which is repeated by Saadya and Rashi) that the oracle alludes to an occasion following the fall of Jerusalem in 587 B.C. when Arabs failed to offer proper hospitality to refugees of the Jewish priesthood,[2] the rabbinic commentators do not offer much in the way of traditions concerning its date and circumstances. Ibn Ezra, commenting on the mention of the sword in verse 15, states simply that it is the king of Assyria who has precipitated the flight of the refugees.

Modern commentators are divided on the question of the dating of the oracle. Broadly speaking three periods may be said to have attracted support amongst them;[3] first, Nebuchadrezzar's campaign, usually dated in 589[4] which, according to Jer. xlix, terrified the inhabitants of Dedan and Kedar as well as those of Edom; secondly, the period of

---

1 See above, p. 57.

2 Rashi (on verse 13) also records a similar failure on the part of Arabs to show pity to Jews – this time 'when Assyria exiled my people'.

3 Kaiser is an exception in that he considers that the oracle refers to 'the eschatalogical threat from unnamed enemies from the North'. This represents an extension of his views of the other oracles in the chapter. As no further arguments in their favour are adduced in connexion with this oracle, no further arguments against them are here required or given.

4 E.g. Rosenmüller and Cheyne, *I.B.I.*

the fall of Babylon in 539;[1] thirdly, the Assyrian period,[2] and more particularly the Arabian campaigns of Sargon (715) and Sennacherib (some time before 691).[3]

The criteria by which any one of the periods is selected are fundamentally literary; that is to say, the view taken by critics of the relationship of the Arabian oracle to other oracles in the chapter or elsewhere in the bible largely determines their view of its date (so e.g. Wildberger).

Nebuchadrezzar's Palestinian campaign of 589 B.C.

Cheyne (*I.B.I.*) is inclined to emphasize the fact that the oracle (verses 13–17) is juxtaposed to a prophecy apparently concerned with Edom. In this connexion, like Rosenmüller, he notes that Jer. xlix also mentions, along with Edom, the tribes of Dedan and Kedar as fearing the chastening hand of Nebuchadrezzar. He concludes that Isa. xxi 11–17, like Jer. xlix, refers to the situation following Zedekiah's revolt against Babylon, when, in 589 B.C., Nebuchadrezzar advanced into Syria/Palestine.[4] To the possible objection that there is in the Dumah oracle no trace of the anti-Edomite feeling which one would expect at this time, Cheyne is content to emphasize that Edom was certainly an ally of Zedekiah of Judah shortly before 587,[5] and that the Dumah oracle is likely to be pre- rather than post-exilic because it displays an 'equilibrium of feeling . . . which, if it prevents cordiality, not less forbids positive hostility'.

Cheyne's arguments are open to two objections. First, the

1 E.g. Duhm, Marti, Gray and Galling.
2 E.g. Cheyne, *P.I.*; Delitzsch; D.K.; Procksch; Kissane.
3 Erlandsson (pp. 94ff) views the oracle in the light of the Arabian campaigns. However, he adduces no exegetical or literary critical arguments in favour of doing so. He is content to quote with favour Procksch's statement to the effect that in the book of Isaiah the Assyrians are the foe par excellence ('bieten sich im Jesajabuch wider die Assyrer an').
4 Cf. *C.A.H.*, III, pp. 213f. We have no indication from Babylonian records of an attack by Nebuchadrezzar upon Edom, though Josephus, citing Berosus, refers to a campaign undertaken by that king against the Arabs (*Contra Apion* I 19). The general reliability of this notice seems now to be confirmed by Babylonian records; see Wiseman, *Chronicles*, p. 70; cf. pp. 31ff. Here it is stated that a campaign of plunder against the Arabs was undertaken in 599–598 – in the sixth year of Nebuchadrezzar. It is not essential to Cheyne's argument that Nebuchadrezzar should have invaded Edom and Arabia in 589, for he is not committed to the view that the oracle is a *vaticinium ex eventu*; it is enough that these countries should have been threatened at this time.
5 See, with *C.A.H.*, III, Jer. xxviif.

weakness of the argument that the 'Aramaic colouring' of Isa. xxi 11–17 precludes a date earlier than Nebuchadrezzar's time has been exposed by Procksch.[1] Secondly, where Jer. xlix is concerned, the balance of scholarly opinion may be held to favour the view that this chapter, containing as it does material found also in e.g. Obadiah, is a composite work[2] (as is Jer. xlviii) which contains material found in Isa. xvf. On the further question whether these oracles of Jeremiah are dependent upon Obadiah and Isaiah, opinion is divided. It is possible to argue that the authors of Jer. xlviiif on the one hand, and of the relevant chapters of Isaiah and of Obadiah on the other, have all made use of older prophetic material.[3] At any rate, it is clear that Jer. xlix cannot be cited as an independent and contemporary witness in support of the supposition that Isa. xxi 13–17 is concerned with a threat by Nebuchadrezzar to Judah's southern neighbours.[4] For, apart from the question of the contrived character of Jer. xlix, Isa. xxi 13–17 makes no mention of Nebuchadrezzar, whereas Jer. xlix (at least in the case of Kedar) explicitly does so.

To return for a moment to the question of the relationship between Isaiah's foreign oracles and those of Jer. xlviiif, certain considerations may suggest that the balance of probability favours the literary dependence of the latter upon the former. Thus, in Jer. xlix there are verses (8a and 30a) similar in sentiment if not identical in vocabulary to Isa. xxi 13;[5] there is also the close association of Dedan with Edom in both oracles. Further, there are verses in Jer. xlix which are word for word common to verses in Obadiah.[6] These considerations suggest

---

1 See pp. 78f. above. D.K. also discount such arguments.
2 Whether or not there is a kernel of authentic words of Jeremiah is disputed; cf. the commentaries of e.g. Volz and Rudolph.
3 See e.g. J. Bright, *Jeremiah*. Cf. on Isaiah xvf esp. D.K.
4 Cheyne, in fact, introduces his argument with an acknowledgement that he is assuming Jeremiah's authorship.
5 The argument is not affected by Bach's attempt to attribute all such statements to the formal *genre* 'Aufforderung zum Flucht'. For both authors have used such statements (whatever their form) specifically and strikingly in connexion with the Dedanites.
6 For recent discussion of the relationship between Obadiah and Jer. xlix, see Rudolph in *K.A.T.* xiii 2, p. 297, and H. W. Wolff, pp. 20ff. Rudolph takes the view that Obadiah is earlier than Jer. xlix; but both he and Wolff consider it likely that the two are dependent upon an earlier common source (for Wolff that source is specifically oral tradition).

strongly that Jer. xlix is a composite work, that it is dependent upon Obadiah and that it alludes to Isa. xxi (cf. Delitzsch (1)). With this conclusion two other considerations appear to agree; first, Isa. xxi 13f is manifestly a coherent unity and consequently Jer. xlix, which on other grounds is judged a composite work, is best seen as a conscious reflexion of it. Secondly, scholars are generally inclined to accept that Jer. xlviii is dependent upon Isa. xvf.[1] If, then, Jer. xlviii is dependent upon Isa. xvf, it is not unlikely that Jer. xlix reflects Isa. xxi 13f.

Because the argument of Rosenmüller and Cheyne rests upon a comparison of Isaiah's Arabian oracle with Jer. xlix as an independent and contemporary witness to reactions amongst Judah's southern neighbours *c.* 589 B.C., it must be judged implausible. On the contrary, examination of their argument and of the nature of Jer. xlix indicates that Isa. xxi antedates this work and provides elements which its author was inclined to use (see chapter 3 below).

The fall of Babylon in 539 B.C.

Duhm, Marti and Gray may be regarded as typical of those who adopt the theory that the Arabian oracle (i.e. verses 13–15 alone) belongs to the period of the fall of Babylon in 539. For all three scholars considerable importance attaches to the judgement that the oracle was written by the author of verses 1–10. For Duhm this is undoubtedly the case; both oracles present vivid pictures, and here the prophet relates a vision of the Dedanites pursued by Persian horsemen. For Marti, metre and structure are the same in verses 1–10 and 13–15; consequently the two oracles are to be attributed to the same author, though possibly the Arabian oracle is slightly later. The oracle follows admirably upon one which recounts the fall of Babylon and it indicates that the seer did not expect that the Persians would deal favourably with those peoples who had hitherto been subject to Babylon.[2] Marti also approves of Duhm's suggestion that the author is likely to have dwelt in

---

1 See the commentaries of Duhm, Rudolph and Weiser. For a judicious statement of this case and for further references, see Wildberger, pp. 605ff.

2 Wildberger (p. 801) attributes to Marti the view that the Persian army sought to secure the caravan routes of Arabia for the empire. This, however, Marti does not actually say.

southern Palestine and as a consequence was naturally sympathetic to Judah's Arab neighbours.

Gray's approach is similar to that of Duhm and Marti, though it is very much more tentative. He is inclined to suppose that the piece is from the same hand as verses 1–10 and that it probably relates the contents of a vision rather than an actual historical flight. For Gray the Dedanites are likely to be fleeing from Babylon. Arriving with the expectation that they would conduct their usual business affairs they find instead Babylon threatened by the Persians and consequently they take to the caravan routes in flight.

Two modifications of this general approach are proposed by Galling and Wildberger. Both scholars connect the Arabian oracle closely with the preceding Babylonian one, but Galling considers that the very great distance (800 km) between Babylon and Teima precludes the generally accepted notion that Persian mounted detachments[1] should have pursued the Dedanites over such a distance through the desert immediately following the fall of Babylon. The danger zone for the Dedanites, if they are pictured as originally in and around Babylon, is Babylon and not the far-off region of Teima. Further, even if so long a flight is in the prophet's mind, why is his advice concerned only with the later stage of it (i.e. that around Teima)? For Galling, it is much more likely that the prophecy (like those that precede it) is to be dated soon after Nabonidus's departure from Teima in 545. In this situation, the Babylonian garrisons left behind by Nabonidus are likely to have been involved in skirmishes with the native Arabs, who, following that monarch's departure, may be presumed to have made bids for freedom. For Galling, then, the threat from which the Dedanites are pictured as fleeing consists of Babylonians (or their allies) rather than Persians, and their flight is confined from beginning to end to the deserts around Teima.

Galling's criticisms of what he regards as the generally accepted view of the Arabian oracle (i.e. what has been described above as the view of Duhm, Marti and Gray) are cogent, and, in their own right, worthy of acceptance. On the other hand, his own understanding of the background to the

---

1 He notes that nothing in the text suggests such mounted troops.

oracle rests upon various inferences and above all upon the assumption that the oracles of the chapter, like that of verses 1–10, concern the (imminent) fall of Babylon in 539. While, then, his criticisms of Duhm, Marti and Gray's view of the oracle are in their own right convincing, his view, like theirs, is ultimately dependent upon a particular understanding of the historical background to Isa. xxi 1–10. If doubts attach to that understanding, Galling's subsequent inferences, however plausible in themselves, are likely to prove erroneous.

Wildberger is content merely to quote the views of Marti and Galling on the Arabian oracle without attempting to judge between them. However, he suggests as a further possibility that the oracle may reflect internal conflicts between the Arabian tribes, and more particularly an attempt by the tribe of Kedar to control and to dominate the trade routes of the area; such an assumption would explain why verses 16f (which concern Kedar) were considered a necessary addition by the editor of the chapter. At any rate, as Wildberger inclines to the view that both the Dumah and the Arabian oracles are best understood as belonging to the period after the fall of Babylon, the criticisms of Galling's views mentioned above apply *mutatis mutandis* with equal force to his.

The Assyrian period

Those commentators[1] who understand the Arabian oracle to have as its background the period of the Assyrian attacks upon North Arabia do so because they believe that it is closely related to the Dumah (Edom) oracle which precedes it and with the Kedar oracle (verses 16f) which follows it. Where the latter text is concerned, comparison is made with Isa. xvi 13f where virtually identical words are used as the substance of an additional revelation about Moab. The words as they occur in Isa. xvi 13f are regarded as genuinely Isaianic by all these commentators, and consequently they incline to the view that the words of xxi 16f are also genuine. In both cases the texts have the particular function of elucidating and determining more accurately the contents of the oracles which precede them, whether those oracles are appropriated by Isaiah from

1 E.g. Cheyne, *P.I.*; Delitzsch; D.K.; Procksch; Kissane.

older prophetic material (e.g. Hitzig and D.K.) or whether they are merely earlier poems of the prophet subsequently in need of such elucidation (e.g. Delitzsch and Procksch).

For commentators of this school, therefore, the Moab oracles of Isa. xvf and the Dumah/Arabian oracles of Isa. xxi 11ff have as their background the years 720–710 B.C. and Sargon II's campaigns against South Palestine and North Arabia which can be dated in this period (*C.A.H.* iii, p. 58). Where the words of xxi 16f are concerned, two of the commentators provide particular and differing accounts. First, Dillmann–Kittel regard them as the contents of a revelation to Isaiah himself in which the contents of the Arabian oracle (earlier appropriated and reproduced by Isaiah) were confirmed, the only difference being that Isaiah's own revelation spoke of Kedar (i.e. the main tribe of North Arabia beyond Edom), whereas it was the Dedanites who were mentioned in the oracle which he had earlier appropriated. Secondly, Procksch regards as significant the fact that the Dedanites are the object of Isaiah's sympathy, while the tribe of Kedar is the object of his threat. He suggests, therefore, that the tribe of Kedar were allies of the Assyrians[1] and that it was they in particular who threatened the Dedanites. Isaiah's prophecies indicate his hope that the Dedanites would shortly be freed from the particular menace facing them, as so many small nations would be freed from that of the Assyrians themselves.

Commentators of this school, who, by contrast, believe that Isa. xxi 1–10 has as its background the period of the fall of Babylon in 539, are inclined to emphasize what they regard as the considerable differences between that oracle and those which follow it. Procksch, for example, is at pains to discount the arguments presented by those who see a unity between verses 1–10 and the oracles that follow it. However, the arguments that he in turn produces are unconvincing in character. For example, he notes that revelation comes directly to the prophet in verse 11 (אֵלַי) but through the prophet's *alter ego* in verses 1–10; or again verses 1–10 use the word מצפה while the prophet is called שׁמר in the Dumah oracle.

---

1 He compares Isa. xxii 6 where, he claims, other allies of Assyria are mentioned by name. Some doubts, however, attach to this interpretation of the verse; see below.

Some considerable advantages attach to the view that the Arabian oracle, like the Dumah oracle which precedes it, belongs to the Assyrian period. For the judgement, if it can be sustained by plausible arguments, may in turn have implications for the understanding of the oracle of verses 1–10, and render possible the view that chapter xxi as a whole (or at least an earlier form of it), like chapters xx and xxii before and after it, is to be dated in the last years of the eighth century B.C.

Doubt, however, attaches to one particular link in the argument presented by those scholars who advocate a date in Assyrian times for the Arabian oracle. It is the judgement that verses 16f are genuine (if later) words of Isaiah and the consequent conclusion that the Arabian oracle is to be dated in Assyrian times. The difficulty arises that the initial judgement is entirely unsupported (and perhaps unsupportable) by objective criteria. Indeed another and quite different judgment of the verses concerned has been made, viz. that, being phrased in prose and having a somewhat stereotyped character, they are likely to be later editorial additions to earlier prophecies (whether or not Isaianic).[1] Moreover, it is possible to argue that verses 16f, being in the form of a judgement, are at odds with the apparently sympathetic attitude displayed towards the Arabs in the Arabian oracle.

A comparison more likely to yield arguments in favour of an Assyrian date for the Arabian (and Dumah) oracles is that which has been made between them and the Moab oracles of Isa. xvf.[2] While it must be admitted that the exegesis of Isa. xvf is very uncertain and that the conclusions of the commentators are as tentative as they are varied, there are at least some indications which may suggest a common background. Thus it is possible to detect a note of sympathy towards Moab in these chapters;[3] feelings of solidarity and sympathy too have been detected in the attitude of the Dumah and

---

1 E.g. Wildberger; cf. Duhm, Marti and Fohrer. The exegesis and understanding of Isa. xvi are so uncertain and varied that interpretation of the relationship of verses 13f to what precedes them is here left out of account.
2 So e.g. (briefly) D.K.
3 See esp. xv 1–5 and xvi 8–11. Wildberger regards these sections as old laments over Moab. To him it is unthinkable that they should have been on the lips of Isaiah, but he believes that their sympathetic attitude points to the period between Tiglath-pileser and the end of Judah when all the Palestinian states were, so to speak, in the same boat.

Arabian oracles (so e.g. Wildberger, pp. 798ff). Secondly, there is the use in both the Moabite and the Dumah oracles of the unusual form לֵיל (Isa. xv 1; cf. xxi 11), a form which, as ibn Ezra suggested (see above, pp. 43f), may imply that a particular night is referred to and that the oracles thus indicate the same historical situation. Thirdly, to both has been appended a prose epilogue[1] in wording that is largely identical. As it is virtually certain that the epilogues derive from the same author, it is further likely that their author regarded the preceding oracles as in some sense comparable.

If literary considerations suggest (albeit very tentatively) a common background for the Moab oracles and those of Isa. xxi 11ff the question naturally arises whether Moab, Edom and North Arabia were ever historically the joint object of an attack by a foreign power and at a time when we may suppose that a Judaean prophet might show them at least a modicum of sympathy. The only period when all such conditions were fulfilled was that of the Assyrian attacks on southern Palestine and Arabia at the end of the eighth and the beginning of the seventh centuries B.C. (see above, pp. 78f, and below, pp. 131f).

Verses 16 & 17

The view of those scholars who suppose that this oracle is a genuine (if later) Isaianic addition have been discussed above in relation to the Arabian oracle. It remains here to record two further views of these verses. First, Duhm (followed by Marti) considers that the oracle is an epilogue belonging to the time of Alexander Jannaeus (104–73 B.C.) when Aretas and the Arabs constituted a threat to the Jews.[2] In these circumstances the Jews would have recalled with hope the old prophecy concerning the Arabs (which they attributed to Isaiah – so Marti). Such views of the verse in question have gained little support and telling arguments against them have been set forth, e.g. by Galling.[3]

---

1 I.e. on that view of xvi 13f and xxi 16f.
2 Marti suggests the further possibility that the oracle is to be dated in the time of John Hyrcanus (135–105 B.C.).
3 P. 62. In particular the evidence of Sir. xlix (which witnesses to the close of the prophetic canon in the first decade of the second century B.C.) and of 1QIs[a] (which, dated 100 B.C., contains the whole text of Isaiah) is decisive.

Secondly, Wildberger believes that the verses concerning Kedar were added by a later editor to whom Kedar was of more interest than Duma(t el Gendel),[1] Dedan and Teima. It was not until post-exilic times that Kedar's hegemony was established as far as Palestine and Egypt[2] and their business enterprises brought to them considerable prosperity and power (so, according to Wildberger, the word כבוד). At any time during this period the editor concerned could have added such an oracle in the name of Yahweh (without feeling the need to specify the agents of Kedar's collapse) in order to give expression to Israel's faith that the apparent superiority of her foes would be short-lived. Wildberger's treatment of the similar verses of Isa. xvi 13f is fuller and he there expresses the view that the words in question are redolent of apocalyptic schematization rather than of prophetic pronouncement. Thus, the point of the comparison 'like the years of a hireling'[3] is not to denote the exact computation of a period of time, but rather the miserable quality of a hireling's (and so Israel's) life. Moab itself is for the redactor manifestly a paradigm of a heathen godless nation rather than an historical reality. Even the reference to a remnant (though here expressly a tiny one) is stylized, and it is present because such references were thought to be obligatory.

Much of Wildberger's treatment of these verses (on xvi 13f and on xxi 16f) is speculative and perhaps it is necessarily so. On the other hand, his account suffers from the weakness that, while he inclines to the view that a common author was responsible for both additions, his treatment of xvi 13f appears to differ from that of xxi 16f. In the former case he adopts the view that the words are *quasi*-apocalyptic; in the latter he believes that they refer explicitly (if generally) to one of Israel's post-exilic adversaries. Secondly, his understanding of the *tertium comparationis* כשני שכיר is open to serious objection, for it appears to rest upon the view that the absence of an article prefixed to שכיר precludes the translation 'like the years of the (known class) hireling', but permits the translation 'like hireling

---

1 *Sic ex hypothesi* Wildberger.
2 For the evidence for the latter in an Aramaic inscription of the fifth century B.C., see Rabinowitz in *J.N.E.S.* 15 (1956), 1ff.
3 Wildberger is unable to resolve the question whether hireling ('Tagelohner') or mercenary ('Soldner') is the correct translation of שכיר.

years' ('wie Tagelohnerjahre'), i.e. miserable years. In fact, however, the article (theoretically at least) would equally be required if שכיר were used to convey Wildberger's adjectival sense, for if it does convey such an adjectival sense, its grammatical form is still that of a noun and therefore subject to the usual rules. But theoretical considerations apart, from G.K. 126p it is clear that indeterminate comparisons do exist in biblical Hebrew even if they are rare. Wildberger's argument that כשני שכיר must mean 'like hireling years' is therefore, on grammatical grounds, highly dubious. Wildberger, however, also appeals to Job vii 1f where, he submits, the comparison is clearly concerned with the miserable quality of a hireling's life. With this observation there need be no disagreement. When, however, כשני שכיר follows immediately and explains references to a specific number of years (in Isa. xxi 16, one; in xvi 14, three), the 'misery of life' alluded to can hardly imply anything but that the specified number of years will, for the reason that they are miserable, be counted with very great accuracy.

Wildberger's contention that the period of time specified in Isa. xvi 14 is more akin to apocalyptic schematization than to prophetic pronouncement raises interesting questions concerning the relationship between (later) prophecy and apocalyptic. Mention in Isa. xvi 14, however, of so small a period as three years (and *a fortiori* in Isa. xxi 16 of one year) is hardly consistent with the broader sweep of apocalyptic seasons and epochs.

The two epilogues to xvi and xxi are better regarded as later editorial additions designed to give contemporary relevance to the oracles to which they are appended. It may readily be agreed that reinterpretation of prophecy and the attempt to apply older oracles to later situations is an activity which was to reach its ultimate sophistication in apocalyptic. However, the specific nature and short focus of the epilogues before us indicate that they belong to an earlier rather than to a later state in that particular development.

It is difficult to be sure which historical situation the epilogue of xxi 16f reflects. On the one hand, the period par excellence of Kedar's dominance in North Arabia was the Persian.[1] On the

---

1 So Wildberger, p. 802. For a recent evaluation of the evidence concerning the history of Kedar, see Bartlett, 'From Edomites to Nabataeans', pp. 53ff.

other, the name is perfectly well known from Assyrian military annals and Jer. xlix 28 suggests that Nebuchadrezzar campaigned against the tribe in his campaigns of 589–580.[1] Further, from the point of view of the bible, it is possible that the name 'Kedar', originally a tribal name, was used from at least Jeremiah's time (see ii 10) to denote all the peoples of Arabia (so Gray; see above).

On the view that Isa. xvi 13f comes from the same hand as xxi 16f, a date suitable for both epilogues seems to be necessary. It is possible that Nebuchadrezzar's campaign of 582[2] was the beginning of the end of Moab as a state,[3] for thereafter, in the bible at least, references to that country are literary rather than historical.[4] The period in which earlier oracles concerning Moab are most likely to have been adapted to express judgement against that country is precisely 'the end of the seventh and the beginning of the sixth centuries B.C., when Moab appears to have taunted Judah and even attacked her' (Wiseman, *Peoples*, p. 242). If such considerations are sound, Isa. xvf, as redirected by the epilogue to them, may be contemporary with Ezek. xxv 8–11[5] and Jer. xlviii.[6]

---

1 *C.A.H.*, III (p. 215) is inclined to accept this evidence as likely. For the evidence of Josephus and of Babylonian texts, see p. 92 above.
2 So Josephus (*Antiquities* x 9, 7), who mentions that Nebuchadrezzar's attack on Moab was in the twenty-third year of his reign.
3 See A. H. van Zyl, *The Moabites* (Leiden, 1960), pp. 157ff.
4 Cf. with Wildberger, Ezra ix 1; Neh. xiii 1, 23; Pss. lx 10, lxxxiii 7, cviii 10; Isa. xxv 10f; Dan. xi 41.
5 Zimmerli understands this oracle to reflect the events of 582 B.C.
6 That Jer. xlviii does not contain all the material from Isa. xvf need not tell against this understanding of the two. For Jer. xlviii is manifestly contrived and dependent on other biblical texts. That Jer. xlviii should have omitted passages favourable to Moab from Isa. xvf (e.g. xvi 1, 3–5) is consistent with his way of announcing doom for Moab; cf. Wildberger, p. 606.

3

Verses 1–10

History and Exegesis

Consideration of the text and meaning of the oracles of Isa. xxi and of their exegesis in relation to the historical events of the ancient Near East in the period in and after the eighth century B.C. has shown considerable diversity of opinion among scholars. Indeed it is because uncertainty attends any attempt to determine the meaning and import of so much of the text of this chapter that recourse is had to particular working hypotheses, for only by means of them can any reasonably coherent and satisfactory account of its meaning apparently be given. Thus the mention in verses 1–10 of the fall of Babylon together with an apparent reference to an attacking force of Elamites and Medes often constitutes the necessary initial clue for the construction of what I have called the orthodox critical view of this oracle. On the basis of this clue the orthodox critical school plump for the fall of Babylon at the hands of Cyrus. That is their working hypothesis. It is for them the best bet. In support of it (once it is adopted) various historical arguments are adduced.[1] When a phrase in the text does not apparently match it, it is emended,[2] or a different meaning is postulated for it,[3] or other historical considerations are advanced in explanation.[4] And what is true of the orthodox critical view as a working hypothesis is *mutatis mutandis* often true of alternative accounts of the prophecy, e.g. Cobb's view that the oracle is an Isaianic composition of the eighth century B.C.

The question now arises whether this approach to the oracles of Isa. xxi is in fact the one most likely to lead to the correct understanding of its contents. Fundamentally the approach

---

1 E.g. Galling on the return of Nabonidus from the Arabian desert.
2 E.g. Duhm and Wildberger on אנחתה.
3 E.g. Eitan on אנחתה.
4 E.g. D.K., Duhm and Wildberger on the mention of Medes and Elamites rather than Persians as the agents of Babylon's fall.

103

rests upon the assumption that each of the prophecies[1] reflects one particular historical situation. Is the assumption, however, a valid one? Are we right to find in each of the oracles of Isa. xxi clear and consistent references to any one historical situation? To what extent, moreover, is the scholastic adage *quidquid recipitur recipitur ad modum recipientis* likely to be exemplified in the transmission of these oracles? Thus, for example, if (at least some of) the words of Isa. xxi 1–10 antedate the sixth century B.C., would they not have attained new significance precisely in the sixth century – in the eyes of those who received or read them at that time? And if the fall of Babylon at the hands of Cyrus was, after 539, pre-eminently in the minds of those who received the oracle, is it not reasonable to suppose that indications of their understanding of the prophecy may have survived, whether independently of the text (in e.g. rabbinic traditions) or by the adaptation or even emendation of its words to this end?

That prophecies in fact attained new and very particular significance in the minds of those who later received them may be illustrated from the present study in connexion with the Arabian oracle. I recorded (p. 57) the Talmudic tradition that by allusion the prophecy concerns the plight of Jewish refugees fleeing to Arab territory after the fall of Jerusalem at the hands of Nebuchadrezzar in the sixth century B.C. The presence of this tradition in the Talmud provides us with evidence that that is how the prophecy was interpreted in Jewish circles at a comparatively early date.[2] It was further suggested (p. 57 above) that the particular pointing of one word within the oracle may be an indication that the Massoretes also wished to refer the prophecy to this incident.

What can be documented for the reinterpretation of the Arabian oracle from Talmudic and (perhaps) massoretic traditions may be shown for other Isaianic prophecies within the (consonantal) text of Isaiah itself. For example, there is the well-known interpretation of the prophecy of iii 1f, where the word 'staff', originally clearly a characterization of the

---

1 For some, of course, verses 1–10 consist of more than one prophecy.

2 It is conceivable that this linking of the prophecy with events following the fall of Jerusalem in 587 indicates that the prophecy was already in existence at that time; if that could be established we would have, of course, a *terminus ad quem* for it.

eighth-century-B.C. pillars of Judah's society (thereafter listed), is later interpreted as the 'staff of bread' and the 'staff of water' (i.e. as the necessities of life) removed in the circumstances attending the siege of Jerusalem in 587[1] (Ezek. iv 16, v 16, xiv 13).

Again, and equally well known, there is the gloss added to the words of Isa. vi 13, 'the holy seed is the stock thereof' (R.V.), whereby (what was earlier) an oracle of doom has been modified by a later interpreter so that it should convey a promise of hope for a remnant.[2]

If, then, certain prophecies within the book of Isaiah show evidence of having been reinterpreted and directed to situations later than those to which originally they referred, it is possible that those of chapter xxi reflect a similar process.

If this understanding of the oracles of Isa. xxi is correct, it follows that the fundamental assumption adopted by most modern critics, viz. that each prophecy (as we have it) reflects a single historical situation, is mistaken.

It is readily admitted that much of the argument adduced above is *a priori* in character. Yet argument is necessarily of this sort when basic assumptions are questioned; and particularly so when those assumptions underlie the difficult quest for the elucidation of oracles of such antiquity and obscurity as those of Isa. xxi.

The proof of the pudding, however, is in the eating. Apart from the question of assumptions, we have to consider which understanding of the prophecies of Isa. xxi best fits what we can see of them at present. When it is necessary to judge between two understandings which are mutually irreconcilable, then that which leaves unsolved the smaller number of problems is the more likely to be correct.

An attempt will be made to show that many of the words and phrases of Isa. xxi 1–10 have their origin in the eighth century but that the oracle as a whole attained its final form in the book of Isaiah as a prophecy which portrayed the fall of Babylon at the hands of Cyrus in 539 B.C. The prophecy may

---

1 See Gray, p. 63.
2 See e.g. Gray, p. 111. For further discussion of the later reinterpretation of Isaianic oracles, see D. R. Jones in *Z.A.W.* 67 (1955), 256ff. See also S. Mowinckel, *Prophecy and Tradition* (Oslo, 1946), and E. Nielsen, *Oral Tradition* (London, 1954).

then be regarded as a palimpsest. Its reception and interpretation within the Isaianic tradition give to it its superimposed form and it is this that enables it to speak of that fall of Babylon which was of such immense importance in the history of the Jewish people. Beneath the superimposed form, however, we may catch at least glimpses of earlier prophecies and of the historical circumstances of an earlier age.

This understanding of the nature of Isa. xxi 1–10 has the advantage over those which see in it a single historical background, that it accounts for much that is otherwise obscure or apparently archaic. Further, it has the advantage that it accounts for the unity of thought which has been detected (especially by Delitzsch) between Isa. xxi 1–10 and material in the book of Isaiah which is likely to be genuine. For Delitzsch (1) that unity was to be accounted for on the supposition that Isaiah was himself the author of an oracle which portrayed the fall of Babylon in the sixth century B.C.[1] The unity of thought which Delitzsch originally detected can, however, more satisfactorily be accounted for on the supposition that words of Isaiah were later seen to have their fulfilment in the events of the sixth century.

As has been almost universally recognized, the most likely starting point for the interpretation of the oracles of Isa. xxi is the reference to Elamites and Medes in verse 2. To adherents of the orthodox critical theory, the force of Elamites and Medes who are urged to attack must be identified with the forces of the Persian Cyrus who brought about the end of the Babylonian empire in 539. When the question is asked why Cyrus's forces are here characterized as Elamites and Medes, various considerations are advanced to meet the apparent difficulty. Thus the description is held to reflect the diverse character of Cyrus's empire which comprised Media (conquered in 550–549) and Anshan (formerly part of Elam) of which Cyrus was king.[2] Again it is urged that, while it is historically accurate to describe the conquerors of Babylon as Persians, it was customary in Greece and Egypt as well as elsewhere in the O.T. to refer

---

1 Delitzsch's original argument (1) concerns primarily the 'Fall of Babylon' oracle of xiii f; but he claims for Isa. xxi 1–10 the same marks of genuineness.

2 See pp. 67f. For an indication of the uncertain character of this argument, see Barnes, p. 585n.

to the Persians as Medes.[1] Where the term 'Elam' is concerned, it is also urged that there is clear evidence of the continued existence of Elamite culture and identity within the Persian empire[2] although its separate existence as a nation ceased in 640–639 when Ashurbanipal conquered Susa.

Against such considerations there remain formidable objections. As Barnes observes, Cyrus never styled himself an Elamite nor was he known as such either in the bible or in Persian monuments. While it is true that Isa. xiii 17 and Jer. li 11, 28 mention Medes as agents of the fall of Babylon in 539, in none of these texts is there mention of Elam. It may be added that, where Jer. li is concerned, this is particularly noticeable in verse 27 where there is a list of other kingdoms called to attack Babylon in company with the Medes: 'Ararat, Minni and Ashkenaz' (R.V.). Barnes further observes that in Isa. xliv 28 and xlv 1, where Cyrus is actually mentioned by name, no nationality is assigned to him.

We may agree with Wildberger's assertion that the evidence of the oracle concerning Elam in Jer. xlix, whether that oracle is to be dated in the first year of Zedekiah (as its title suggests – see Rudolph and Weiser) or later (see Fohrer, *Einleitung*), seems to corroborate the external indications[3] that Elam, after the fall of Susa in 639, retained some political identity. On the other hand, as Wildberger also admits, the early exilic prophecy of Ezek. xxxii 17ff[4] tells against the view that Elam was a significant power in the time of the Babylonian exile,[5] for there Elam (verse 24) is listed with Assyria and Meshech-tubal[6] amongst the ghosts of bygone empires lingering in Sheol. In the

---

1 See Wildberger, p. 507. He follows H. Bengtson in (S.) *Fischer Weltgeschichte*, vol. v, p. 37, and Wiseman, *Peoples*, p. 316. It should be noted, however, that Persians, not Medes, are mentioned in Ezek. xxvii 10 and xxxviii 5.
2 Wildberger, pp. 772f.
3 E.g. F. W. König, *Geschichte Elams* (Leipzig, 1931) vol. xxix, 4, and *Reallexikon der Assyriologie*, vol. ii (1938), p. 337.
4 For which see e.g. Zimmerli, ii, *ad loc.*
5 The possibility (and it is no more than that) – see Wiseman, *Chronicles*, p. 36 – that the Babylonian Chronicle refers to a king of Elam as an opponent of Nebuchadrezzar in 596 hardly contradicts this view. If the reading were to be verified, it would not amount to evidence that Elam had at the time more than a residual political identity.
6 I.e. nations of Asia Minor (Phrygia and Cappadocia), known as *Muski* and *Tabal* in Assyrian records (see Luckenbill, ii), who, like Elam, were constant opponents of the Assyrian kings.

light of this evidence it would be very strange for a prophetic writer in exilic times to characterize (even part of) Cyrus's forces as Elamites.

Although Elam was not a significant political power in the sixth century B.C. it most certainly was so, as also were the Medes, in Assyrian times. The latter were formidable opponents of the Assyrian empire from 745 and the beginning of its ascendancy under Tiglath-pileser III. This king campaigned against the Medes (*C.A.H.*, III, pp. 34f), and Sargon II, who called them 'the mightly Medes' (Luckenbill, II, no. 11), was obliged to follow his example. During Sennacherib's reign the Medes continued to present a challenge to Assyria,[1] at that time particularly threatened by Merodach-baladan of Babylon and his Elamite allies. In the end it was the Medes under Cyaxares II who brought about the downfall of Assyria, the Babylonians under Nabopolassar joining them for the final assault on Nineveh in 612 (*C.A.H.* III, pp. 296f).

Elam was, perhaps, Assyria's most important and formidable enemy. From 744 B.C. when Tiglath-pileser III consolidated his empire east of the Tigris as far as the northern borders of Elam (*C.A.H.*, III, p. 34), that country, threatened as it was, became the natural enemy of Assyria. At this time (731) Merodach-baladan, prince of Bit Yakin in South Babylonia, originally subject to Tiglath-pileser, wishing to become king of an independent Babylon, began his tireless and skilful negotiations with the Chaldeans in the south and with the Aramaeans in the north. His purpose was to achieve the necessary prerequisite to his plan – a united Babylonia (*C.A.H.*, III, pp. 47f). Yet his greatest achievement was to enlist the support of the Elamites in his venture, and this apparently he did by offering them very considerable bribes and gifts (Brinkman, pp. 161ff). At the accession of Sargon II in 721 he was ready to throw off the Assyrian yoke and, after the battle of Dēr in 720, when Elamites caused the Assyrians to withdraw, he achieved his object. Thereafter he reigned for twelve years until 709 when Sargon ousted him and caused him to flee to his home in Bit Yakin. In 703, shortly after the year of Sennacherib's accession to the Assyrian throne (705), Merodach-baladan regained the Babylonian

---

1 See Luckenbill, II, no. 238, and note particularly the phrase 'to the yoke of my rule I made them submit'.

throne and again sought Elamite military aid to ward off the expected attack on him by Sennacherib. On this occasion 'not only do the Elamites seem to have provided the majority of the troops fighting on the Babylonian side, but...an Elamite commander actually directed the combined army' (Brinkman, p. 165). It should be noted here that Merodach-baladan's embassy to Hezekiah of Jerusalem (2 Kings xx 12–19; Isa. xxxix) may have taken place at this time, and it is likely that his intention was to mount a concerted rising against Assyria in the west (with the aid of such kings as Hezekiah) as well as in Babylon itself. In the event, his unpopularity in Babylon caused its inhabitants to try to forestall his seizing the throne, with the result that he had to act earlier than he had intended (703), (*C.A.H.*, III, p. 63). At all events, Sennacherib's army won the ensuing battle and, after a rule of only nine months, Merodach-baladan fled to the southern swamplands. Sennacherib entered Babylon to a friendly reception.

In 700 B.C. Merodach-baladan fled to Elam before an Assyrian army (led by one of Sennacherib's sons – *C.A.H.*, III, p. 65) whose function was to subdue finally Bit Yakin and its Chaldean inhabitants. He was not heard of again and it is presumed that he died in exile. Thereafter, continued intrigue between the Chaldean Mushezib-marduk, a later anti-Assyrian ruler of Babylon, and the Elamites culminated in the bloody battle of Khalule (*C.A.H.*, III, p. 68) which marked the beginning of the end for the anti-Assyrian Chaldean party in Babylon. Though the battle of Khalule was indecisive, Elam was thereafter in a state of weakness because of the illness of her king, and consequently Sennacherib was able in 689 to deal with Babylon unhindered. The troops sacked and looted the city and 'the gods dwelling therein – the hands of my people took them and they smashed them'.[1]

In connexion with this outline of the history of relations

---

[1] Luckenbill, II, no. 340. Boutflower and Erlandsson note that the word 'smashed' (*ušabbiru*) is cognate to that used in Isa. xxi 9; Boutflower regards this as evidence that this part of the prophecy concerns the fall of Babylon in 689 on the grounds that a prophecy is 'interpreted by its fulfilment'. Erlandsson merely notes the correspondence without further comment. It seems to me, however, that little can be made of this correspondence other than that the Bavian inscription confirms that Assyrians did smash (even) Babylonian gods, whereas Cyrus apparently smashed no one's.

between Elam, Babylon and Assyria in the eighth century B.C., two further points should be made. First, it is abundantly clear that various Aramaean peoples living to the east of the Tigris were throughout this period actively involved on the side of the anti-Assyrian Chaldeans. Indeed since as early as 818 B.C. these peoples had sided with Babylon against Assyria (*C.A.H.*, III, p. 27). As has been stated above, Merodach-baladan's first diplomatic missions were concerned with enlisting their support (*ibid.* p. 48), and by the time of the revolt in the years following 705 he could count on them (*ibid.* p. 62; cf. Brinkman, p. 164). They were likewise present amongst the forces raised by Mushezib-marduk in 691 (*C.A.H.*, III, p. 68).

Secondly, as Brinkman has concluded (p. 164) from a survey of the evidence, it was the Elamites who undertook most of the actual fighting with Assyria; Merodach-baladan himself always seemed to avoid direct confrontation with them.

As Erlandsson has said, 'It seems obvious that the oracle of Isa. xxi 1–10 with the names Elam, Media and Babylon harmonizes very well with the historical actualities around 700 B.C.' It should be noted that Erlandsson's conclusion is a restatement of what had been suggested for the oracle by other scholars at an earlier time.[1] Now Kleinert's statement of the case for an eighth-century-B.C. date for the prophecy rested on the assumption that the Elamites and Medes of verse 2b were, like the Elamites and men of Kir in Isa. xxii 6, loyal vassals serving in the Assyrian army. Where Isa. xxii 6 is concerned, scholars of the orthodox critical school are largely in agreement with Kleinert's view of the matter. For Isa. xxi 2, however, they believe the assumption to be entirely out of place, for, as Dillmann–Kittel observe (see above, p. 67), Elam and Media, represented in the prophecy as attacking Babylon (see verses 2 and 9), were at that time *enemies* of Sargon and *allies* of Babylon.

With this objection to Kleinert's interpretation there can be nothing but complete agreement. It is unthinkable that the author of an oracle in the last decade of the eighth century B.C. would characterize an Assyrian army as (consisting of) Elamites and Medes.[2]

---

1 On Kleinert, Cheyne etc., see above.

2 The objection is quite as telling when applied to modifications of the original statement such as that of Barnes; see p. 71 above.

The question, however, remains: why is the Assyrian army attacking Jerusalem in Isa. xxii 6[1] described as comprising Elamites and men of Kir (i.e. Aramaeans[2])? The usual explanation that Elamites and Aramaeans served as vassals in the Assyrian army is based, so far as I am aware, purely on speculation for which there is no evidence.[3] Further, if it is unthinkable that Elamites (and Medes) should have served as loyal vassals of Assyria in her attack on Babylon at the end of the eighth century (Isa. xxi 2), then it is equally unthinkable that Elamites and Aramaeans should have done so in her attack on Hezekiah of Jerusalem (Isa. xxii 6).

There remains an alternative way of understanding both Isa. xxi 2b and xxii 6 as authentic texts which reflect accurately the circumstances of the eighth century B.C. They may be understood as quotations which are reproduced and incorporated in the respective oracles. It was noted above (p. 15) that ibn Ezra (and, apparently independently, Erlandsson) regard Isa. xxi 2b as a quotation of the shouts of soldiers urging each other to battle, and his view, like so much in the rabbinic commentaries, may depend upon ancient tradition.

If Isa. xxii 6 is indeed a quotation, it is incorporated into the oracle (presumably by Isaiah) in order vividly to represent the initial mistaken judgement of Hezekiah's Jerusalem. News of Merodach-baladan's mobilization of the Aramaeans and his successful enlisting of the support of Elam had been on the lips of Jerusalem's inhabitants. On it they had pinned their hopes for deliverance from Assyria. The actual result of this mistaken reliance upon foreign powers is depicted in the next verse (7): 'And it came to pass (ויהי – i.e. the result of all this is) that thy choicest valleys were full of chariots, and the horsemen set themselves in array at the gate' (R.V.). In other words, Sennacherib's siege of 701–700 was, according to Isaiah, the inevitable result of Jerusalem's sinful reliance upon foreign military power.

1 The oracle is usually regarded as substantially Isaianic and reflecting Sennacherib's siege of Jerusalem in 700 B.C.
2 Cf. with most commentaries Amos ix 7.
3 An alternative solution to the problem is to attribute the verse to a later redactor who mistakenly supposed that Elamites were among the besiegers of Jerusalem; so e.g. Marti. There is, however, no good reason, apart from the difficulty at present under discussion, to deny the authenticity of the verse.

This understanding of Isa. xxii 6 has the merit that it fits perfectly the situation at the end of the eighth century B.C. as we know it from the Assyrian sources and it is entirely consistent with the thought and style of Isaiah of Jerusalem (see p. 18 above).

The phrase 'Go up, Elam, etc.' in Isa. xxi 2b may be viewed as a very similar quotation whose incorporation in the oracle vividly depicts the attitude of the inhabitants of Jerusalem. Relying on Babylon and its king (see Isa. xxxix 1) they pin their hopes on his Elamite and Median forces,[1] urging them to victory against the Assyrians. The reaction of Isaiah to this attitude on the part of his countrymen is related in the following verse (3) . 'Therefore (עַל כֵּן) are my loins filled with anguish...' His message from Yahweh is that Babylon will fall to the Assyrians and reliance upon her is as foolish as reliance upon any other foreign power. Again, this understanding of the all-important phrase has the merit that it fits the historical circumstances admirably, and is consistent with the thought of Isaiah of Jerusalem.[2]

If this interpretation of Isa. xxi 2b is correct, then two assumptions of the orthodox critical view must be abandoned: first, the assumption that the agents of the fall of Babylon (verse 9) are named in verse 2b; secondly, the assumption that the speaker of the command in verse 2b, 'Go up, Elam, etc.', is Yahweh and that, consequently, the command belongs to the prophetic form 'summons to war' (*Aufforderung zum Kampf*).[3]

The arguments rehearsed above attempt to show that the all-important phrase 'Go up, Elam, etc.' belongs originally to the earlier level of the palimpsest that constitutes Isa. xxi. It is also suggested, however, that the words were later seen to have their fulfilment in the fall of Babylon at the hands of Cyrus in 539. To this interpretation of the prophecy rabbinic tradition

---

1 The mention of Medes may be a further accurate reflexion of the circumstances, for the Medes did pose a threat to the Assyrians; see above, pp. 108 ff. On the other hand, the use of the term may here constitute a parallelistic synonym for 'Elam'.

2 It will be recalled that the distress of the prophet at the news of the fall of Babylon constituted an important objection to the orthodox critical view; on the present interpretation it is entirely understandable.

3 So Bach.

bears ample witness (see above, pp. 14ff) and indeed it is in accord with the teaching of the great exilic writer Deutero-Isaiah. For here, within the Isaianic tradition itself, is set forth the argument from prophecy. Yahweh, unlike the Babylonian idols, is God, for he acts in history, and before he acts he tells his witnesses of his intentions so that they may perceive his purpose (see e.g. Isa. xli 22ff, xlii 11ff, xliv 6ff, and esp. xlv 20ff). The prophecies to which Deutero-Isaiah is referring, and on the fulfilment of which he bases his case, are likely to comprise material such as Isa. xxi – material that has come down from Assyrian times.

On the basis of the assumption that Isa. xxi 2b was thus interpreted by late exilic or early post-exilic readers, two further points may be made. First, in the new situation the archaic and anachronistic character of the words will not have diminished the force of the revelation. The reverse is likely to have been the case; reference to the Persian Cyrus under the names of Elam and Media will have served to emphasize the mysterious consistency and power of Yahweh whose words are revealed in past history yet find fulfilment in contemporary events.

Secondly, the reinterpretation of the words will have invested the phrase as a whole with a new form and significance. Now, indeed, linked with the news of the fall of Babylon (verse 9), it becomes the formal summons to war (*Aufforderung zum Kampf*), a feature which became so common in exilic prophecies.[1]

It has been suggested that Isa. xxi 1–10 is a sort of palimpsest and that many of its words and phrases may be traced back to the eighth century B.C. and to Assyrian times. On the other hand, it is suggested that the oracle in the form in which we have it was seen to have its fulfilment in the fall of Babylon in 539 B.C. The question arises whether there is any collateral evidence to corroborate this suggestion. In answer to that question, attention may be directed to the prophecy of the fall of Babylon in Jer. lf. It is widely believed that this prophecy is an exilic composition which, like other foreign oracles in

---

1 Cf. with Bach Jer. xlvi 9; xlix 31; l 14f, 29; li 11, 27.

Jer. xlvi–li, is dependent upon earlier prophecies.[1] More particularly its dependence upon the book of Isaiah, and especially upon Isa. xiii f,[2] is very widely accepted. As one small but telling illustration, we may cite the use, in Jer. l 29 and li 5, of the characteristically Isaianic title of Yahweh, 'the Holy One of Israel'. Although dependence upon Isa. xiii f has been widely noticed, attention has not generally been given to the striking points of contact between these chapters and the oracle of Isa. xxi 1–10.[3] The more obvious of those points of contact (i.e. where there is at least partial verbal identity) may be listed as follows:

(1) li 48, 53, 55f. In all these four verses the 'spoiler' (R.V.) is to ravage Babylon, whether the 'spoiler' is Yahweh himself (55) or his agents (48, 53, 56). Cf. the use of the word *šdd* in Isa. xxi 2.

(2) li 8. In this verse the fall of Babylon is announced in words identical (נפלה בבל) to those in Isa. xxi 9.

(3) l 2; li 47, 52. In these verses God's judgement on the graven images of Babylon is recorded; the word פסילים is used in the two latter cases; cf. Isa. xxi 9. It may also be significant that in these verses (47 and 52) the word ארץ occurs after פסילים as it does in Isa. xxi 9, though of course in a quite different sense.

(4) li 33. Babylon is described as 'like a threshing-floor at the time when it is trodden'. Cf. the use of the same word (גרן) in Isa. xxi 10.

Since on other grounds Jer. lf is to be regarded as dependent upon the prophecies of Isaiah, the most likely explanation of such verbal correspondences is that the author of this material made use of Isa. xxi 1–10. To that conclusion at least two further resemblances[4] between the texts (but without exact verbal agreement) may also point. They are:

(1) l 2, 'Babylon is taken' (R.V.) (נלכדה בבל); cf. Isa. xxi 9.

(2) li 1, 'a destroying wind' (R.V.) (רוח משחית); cf. Isa. xxi 1.

---

1 See e.g. the commentaries of Rudolph and Weiser.

2 For a recent treatment, see Erlandsson, pp. 154ff.

3 An exception is Delitzsch (1) who initially believed that Jeremiah 'was acquainted with this oracle'.

4 Other cases where Jer. lf possibly alludes to Isa. xxi 1–10 are mentioned in the commentary below.

Jer. lf is usually dated at a time just prior to Cyrus's capture of Babylon,[1] and its function seems to have been to set forth Yahweh's imminent action in destroying Babylon and enabling the return of the exiles to Judah. That its author has made use of the oracle Isa. xxi 1–10 is thus an independent indication that Jews of the late exilic period saw in the history of their times a fulfilment of (some part of) the words of Isa. xxi 1–10.

It should here be noted that the author of Jer. lf has incorporated interpretative changes or amplifications to the prophecies which he has used. Thus, Jeremiah's prophecy (vi 22–4) depicts a foe from the north who threatens 'the daughter of Zion': in l 41–3 it is 'the daughter of Babylon' who becomes the object of the same threat. In Jer. vi 24 it is 'we' (*sc.* the Judaeans) who are terrified by the threat, whereas in l 43 it is the king of Babylon. Again, as an example of the author's treatment of an Isaianic prophecy, Jer. li 53 may be cited. In Isa. xiv 13 'I will ascend into heaven (השמים אעלה), I will exalt my throne above the stars of God' (R.V.) becomes, in Jer. li 53 'Though Babylon should mount up to heaven (תעלה בבל השמים), and though she should fortify the height of her strength…' (R.V.).

The same treatment, as one would expect, is to be discerned in the use that is made of Isa. xxi 1–10. Where Isa. xxi 10 speaks of (?) Israel in the vocative as 'my threshing' and as 'the corn of my threshing-floor' (R.V.), Jer. li 33 explicitly regards the daughter of Babylon as 'like a threshing-floor at the time when it is trodden' (R.V.). Isaiah's image is, however, interpreted further in Jer. li 33 where the statement 'yet a little while, and the time of harvest shall come for her' (R.V.) is added.

If, then, there is evidence to the effect that the author of Jer. lf has adapted (at least some of) the material in Isa. xxi 1–10 to the situation of his own times, that constitutes an external indication in favour of the view suggested on other grounds above, that the same process took place within the Isaianic tradition itself and that the text of Isa. xxi 1–10, as we have received it, reflects that process.

It remains to present a translation and annotation of the text

---

1 See e.g. Rudolph and Weiser.

of Isa. xxi 1–10 in accordance with this understanding of it. Before that is done, some preliminary observations must be made:

1. It cannot be emphasized too strongly that, on the view of the text which has been presented above, any attempt systematically to distinguish the eighth-century original text from the sixth-century interpreted text is fraught with very considerable uncertainty, and consequently speculation must inevitably be used.

2. If the author of Jer. lf made use of Isa. xxi 1–10, he probably made use of the original text and not of the reinterpreted text. For the reinterpreted text of Isa. xxi 1–10 must have derived its form *ex hypothesi* at a date not so different from that of Jer. lf.

3. It seems unlikely that Jer. lf contains material which can be regarded as *vaticinia ex eventu*.[1] It is possible (see below on verse 5) that the reinterpreted text of Isa. xxi 1–10 contains at least one such *vaticinium*. On that assumption, the reinterpreted text of Isa. xxi 1–10 is later than that of Jer. lf.

4. At all events, whether Jer. lf and the reinterpreted text of Isa. xxi 1–10 are contemporary or not, the former text, being separate from and fuller than the latter, may in places provide clues for use in the attempt to recover the original text of Isa. xxi 1–10.

5. References to pages in the commentary which follows are, unless otherwise stated, references to preceding pages of this work.

Translation and Commentary

Verse 1

Eighth century

Oracle from the wilderness.[a] *A storm,*[b] *sweeping along like whirlwinds in the Negeb, has come*[c] *from the wilderness, from a terrible land.*

a. The title is read משא ממדבר (p. 7). It is likely to be later in date than the oracle itself, but probably antedates the sixth century B.C. (see below).

b. ים is taken to mean 'storm, wind' (pp. 9f) and to be the

---

[1] See again the commentaries of Rudolph and Weiser.

subject of the verb בא. It is possible that the LXX and Peshitta are witnesses to this way of interpreting the verse (p. 7). Jer. li 1 (רוח משחית) may also preserve an echo of this motif (cf. p. 114).

c. בא is probably to be understood as a perfect rather than as a participle (p. 7n).

The storm is a parable or sign of Yahweh's revelation of his will;[1] the contents of the revelation are described in the verses that follow (pp. 9f).

Sixth century

In Jer. li 42 the sea is said to come up upon Babylon (עלה על בבל הים). With this motif verse 55 of the same chapter may be compared. On the assumption that Jer. li is dependent upon Isa. xxi, Jer. li 42 may constitute evidence that the word ים (understood as 'sea') was taken to be an agent of Babylon's fall. With this view the evidence presented by the Targum to Isa. xxi 1 may be consistent (p. 7n above).

On the other hand, Jer. li 13 (cf. Jer. l 38), 'O thou that dwellest upon many waters, (...thine end is come)', may be understood as an indication of an alternative interpretation of ים, viz. that it was read as an absolute in the expression מדבר־ים 'desert of the sea'. This then becomes a name for Babylon which is both descriptive of its geographical features (pp. 5ff) but also proleptic of its fate (cf. ibn Ezra and Delitzsch; pp. 5–6 above). For while the sea is an agent of Babylon's destruction in Jer. li 42, verse 43 states that Babylon will eventually become a dry land and a desert (ציה וערבה). The name מדבר־ים coined for Babylon consequently forms a suitable title for the sixth-century form of the oracle.

On this view of the verse, it would appear at first sight that, because ים was read as part of the title, there would have remained no expressed subject of the verb בא. On the other hand, as has been indicated above, Jer. li 42 may constitute evidence that the word ים, understood as 'the sea' and perhaps regarded as a symbol of invading armies,[2] was also taken to be the subject of the verb בא. That is to say, it seems likely that the word ים in the text of Isa. xxi 1 was interpreted twice: first

---

1 Cf. perhaps Saadya's understanding of the phrase (p. 8 above).
2 Cf. B.D.B., p. 411, and Targum to Isa. xxi 1 (p. 7n above).

as a part of the emended title, and secondly as the subject of the main verb בא.

Oracle, Desert of the Sea. The sea, like whirlwinds sweeping along the Negeb, has come (sc. *upon Babylon*) *from the wilderness, from a terrible (distant) land.*

The reference is to the threat to Babylon posed by the Medes and Persians. They are seen as coming from a terrible, distant land (pp. 10f) by way of the desert between Babylon and the Persian sea (p. 7).

Verse 2a

Eighth century

A harsh vision is told to me: the treacherous deals treacherously and the devastator devastates.

The epigrammatic contents of the harsh vision may be paraphrased in order to bring out its meaning: 'Treacherous rebellion is afoot – but its inevitable result is crushing devastation.' The reference of the term הבוגד (pp. 11f) is to the parties of the anti-Assyrian alliance headed by Merodach-baladan, or perhaps to this king himself. In any case Hezekiah and Judah were firmly involved in these machinations. The term השודד (pp. 12ff) denotes Sennacherib or the Assyrians, whose response to the rebellion will involve swift and brutal repression.

Sixth century

In Jer. li 55f Yahweh is said to be the devastator of Babylon (שודד) and in verse 53 devastators (שדדים) are said to come upon her (יבואו לה). Further, in the book of Jeremiah (p. 13) Babylon is characterized as the devastator (שודד) of Jerusalem. It is likely then that the epigrammatic words were interpreted in the sixth century to mean that Babylon, once the devastator, is herself to be devastated.[1] With this interpretation the words of Isa. xxxiii 1 are consistent and, being late, they may be a reflection of it (cf. also Hab. ii 8). It should be recalled here that the Targum to Isa. xxi 1 reflects this (re)interpretation of the verse, having for the second word in each pair a passive verb (pp. 12f above).

[1] Cf. Ps. cxxxvii 8, where הַשְּׁדוּדָה (בבל) was probably originally הַשָּׁדוֹדָה (בבל); so e.g. B.H.³

As there is no manuscript or versional evidence (apart from the Targum, for which see above, pp. 12f) to indicate that any of the words of the saying was read as a passive, and in the light of Jer. li 25 where Yahweh is the subject of the active participle שׁוֹדֵד, it is probable that in the sixth century B.C. the phrase הַשּׁוֹדֵד שׁוּדָד was understood *quasi* impersonally: 'There is one who is devastating the (erstwhile) devastator' (cf. Rashi; p. 13 above).[1]

Although such an account of the phrase הַשּׁוֹדֵד שׁוֹדֵד is reasonably satisfactory, it is less easy to offer an estimate as to the way in which הַבּוֹגֵד בּוֹגֵד was interpreted. For the word is not found in Jer. li and is not predicated elsewhere in the O.T. of Babylon. On the other hand, if the phrase הַשּׁוֹדֵד שׁוֹדֵד was reinterpreted in the way suggested above, it is not implausible to suggest that the adjoining phrase הַבּוֹגֵד בּוֹגֵד was seen to depict an aspect of the shameful conduct of Babylon as a world power which now, in her turn, she was to experience. Two of the ancient versions (p. 12) detected in the word overtones of oppression and such may have been generally a corollary of the meaning 'treachery' that is clearly attested for the word.

A harsh vision is told to me: there is one dealing treacherously with her who dealt treacherously (with us); there is one devastating her who devastated (us).

The vision is likely to have been understood to be harsh for Babylon (cf. the rabbinic commentators, p. 13 above). The agent of the vengeance exacted on Babylon is thought to be Yahweh; cf. Jer. li 55.

Verse 2b

Eighth century

'*Go up Elam: show hostility, Media.*'[a] *Bring an end to*[b] *all quietness.*[c]

a. The words are a quotation of the sentiments expressed by the people of Judah at the prospect of Babylonian-inspired

---

1 It is unlikely that Isa. xxxiii 1 can be cited in support of an argument that the second word in each pair was reinterpreted as a passive. For while a passive form of שׁדד is found there (תּוּשַּׁד 'thou wilt be devastated'), when the same construction is sought for the verb בגד which follows, there is a reversion to the (equivalent) impersonal third person plural active construction (יִבְגְּדוּ בָךְ 'men will deal treacherously with thee').

rebellion against Assyria. Elam and Media are Merodach-baladan's allies and principal fighting force, and they are urged to attack Assyria (pp. 14f, 111ff).

b. הַשְׁבִּתוּ is read (pp. 17ff). It seems unlikely that the sudden introduction of a first person singular subject (? referring to Yahweh) belongs to the earlier text. On the other hand, such an understanding of the text is precisely of a sort with later reinterpretation. The imperative phrase (השבתו) may be taken to indicate the inevitable result of the policy of rebellion indicated by the quotation; cf. the imperative of Isa. vi 9f.[1] The sense of the argument is: 'your reliance upon rebellious intrigue will have the consequence that you will destroy all possibility of retaining or adopting that quiet, trustful waiting upon Yahweh which is proper'; cf. e.g. Isa. vii 9, viii 5ff.

c. A noun derived from the root נוח is read. Perhaps נַחַת or (with prosthetic א) the form אֲנָחָה[2] may be posited.

Sixth century

Go up, Elam; besiege, Media. I have brought an end to all sighing.

Yahweh is the subject of the first person singular verb and is also understood to be the speaker of the imperative phrase. He summons the Persian empire (under archaic names) to attack Babylon (cf. Jer. l 9; li 11, 27ff) and he announces the final ending of the oppression (the sighing) of the Babylonian exile (pp. 16f).

Verse 3

Eighth century

Therefore my loins are filled with anguish; pangs have taken hold of me, as the pangs of a woman giving birth: I am so pained that I cannot hear, so dismayed that I cannot see.

עַל כֵּן 'therefore' here denotes consequence (p. 19). The prophet's terror is induced as a consequence of the attitude adopted by the Judaeans (p. 112). For the likely privative sense of מִן, see p. 19.

---

1 For the use of the imperative to denote inevitable consequence, G.K. 110f.
2 Cf. the form הֲנָחָה in Est. ii 18.

Sixth century

There is no discernible change in the text. It is possible, however, that the speaker was at this time interpreted as the Babylonians or their king. See the views of the rabbinic commentators, pp. 19f above.

Verse 4

Eighth century

My heart palpitated (wildly), convulsions have overwhelmed me. The dawn that I longed for has been turned into trembling for me.

For a discussion of the meaning of the words, see pp. 20ff. Dawn, strictly the faint light of dawn, is a symbol for Isaiah of the possibility of salvation for Judah, for which he had fervently hoped. Since king and people had rejected reliance upon Yahweh in favour of alliances with Babylon etc. the bare hope which could be entertained has been forfeited.

Sixth century

The speaker is probably, as in the previous verse, interpreted as the Babylonians or their king. It is possible that נשׁף חשׁקי may have been taken to refer (as a *vaticinium ex eventu*) to the feasting in the city of Babylon mentioned as taking place on the night before its capture.[1] See further on the next verse. In this case the last phrase would be taken to convey the meaning 'My night of rejoicing has been turned into trembling' (pp. 21f).

Verse 5

Eighth century

Men prepare weapons,[a] *they set the watch.*[b] *'Arise, O princes, anoint (your) shields' or 'Arise, O princes, anoint a king.'*[c]

a. עָרֹךְ הַשֻּׁלְחָן is read (see p. 27).
b. See pp. 25, 27. אכול שתה is not part of the eighth-century text.
c. For the alternative translations, see pp. 25ff.

[1] For the view of the rabbinic commentators that the reference is to Belshazzar's feast, see p. 22. It is possible that the reinterpretation of Isa. xxi 5 in the sixth century was a factor in the creation of the story of Belshazzar's feast in Dan. v.

The first two phrases are understood to be a description of the anti-Assyrian military preparations taking place in Judah in Hezekiah's days. The last phrase of the verse is an ironic exhortation on Isaiah's part to the leaders of the state to take part in such preparations. 'Anointing the shield' denotes the preparing of them for use in battle (see pp. 25ff). The alternative translation, presented here as a possibility, might constitute Isaiah's ironic exhortation to the leaders of the conspiracy, to effect the enthronement in Babylon of Merodach-baladan.

Sixth century

Men prepare the tables, and light the torches. There is eating and drinking. 'Arise, O princes, anoint (your) shields.'

It seems likely that the words of the verse have been adapted as a *vaticinium ex eventu* to reflect the circumstances of the fall of Babylon and particularly the feasting at its centre reported also by Herodotus and Xenophon (see p. 63 above). The imperative phrase 'Arise, O princes,...' is presumably understood as an ironic call to the Babylonians to defend themselves (cf. the more descriptive phrase in Jer. li 30, where Babylon's soldiers are represented as totally demoralized).

The phrase אכל שתה may have found its way into the text from the nearby Isa. xxii 13 where it occurs in the context of a description of eighth-century Jerusalem's rejoicing at Sennacherib's failure to take Jerusalem. If this is so, it is possible that the motif of a city feasting and at ease is derived from Isa. xxii 12f and that Babylon's fate in Isa. xxi has been interpreted in the light of it. Such an interpretation might constitute the sort of exact retribution which was seen in the words of Isa. xxi 2a (see p. 118).[1] What Jerusalem suffered, Babylon was to suffer. Cf. Jer. li 35.

Three verses of Jer. lf may possibly reflect the eighth-century text of Isa. xxi (i.e. l 42 and li 11f). In l 42, Babylon's attackers are described as fully armed and ready for their work. The participial form עָרוּךְ is there used. In li 11f Babylon's enemies are bidden in terms compatible with *Aufforderung zum Kampf* to prepare for their attack. There are no exact verbal

---

1 It is unlikely *ex hypothesi* that Isa. xxii was interpreted in the sixth century B.C. solely by reference to events of the last decade of the eighth century.

parallels (e.g. הַחֲזִיקוּ הַמִּשְׁמָר; cf. Isa. xxi 5, צפה הצפית) but the sense is very similar.

It is likely that the references in Jer. li 39 and 57 to Yahweh's imposing upon Babylon's warriors and princes a drunken stupor are derived from such passages as Jer. xxv 15 where Yahweh's cup of anger is referred to (cf. e.g. Rudolph). At any rate the content of these verses is totally different from that of Isa. xxi 5 – even on the view (which is here repudiated) that the latter text in its eighth-century form referred to feasting.

It is very difficult to be sure how the phrase צפה הצפית was interpreted in the sixth century. On the theory here proposed it is likely that the words were taken to denote some aspect of the feast. If they were not interpreted as an indication that the revellers posted watchmen, then the translation 'light the torches' may be adopted on the grounds that it seems to have some support in rabbinic tradition (see p. 25).

Verse 6

Eighth century

Surely thus has the Lord spoken to me: 'Go, station a watchman. Let him recount what he sees.'

The asseverative use of כִּי (B.D.B., p. 472) together with the reference to מצפה suggests a particular link with the preceding verse. The Judaeans set their watch in military preparation (verse 5); but Yahweh too has stationed his watchman (viz. the prophet) who will recount what is actually to happen. It is not necessary to regard the watchman as an *alter ego* of psychological theory (p. 28); rather the use of imagery is figurative (see the views of ibn Ezra and Wildberger, pp. 28f above) and the watchman is none other than Isaiah himself, the recipient of the divine command (אלי).

Sixth century

There is no discernible change in the text. It is difficult to be sure of the way in which the verse might have been interpreted in relation to events of the sixth century. Jer. lf provides no clues, though the sixth-century prophecy of Hab. ii 1-8, which concerns the imminent fall of Babylon, has striking points of similarity both with this verse and verse 8 and may therefore constitute evidence. In particular Hab. ii 1–3 (R.V.):

> I will stand upon my watch, and set me upon the tower, and will look forth to see what he will speak with (or *by*) me and what I shall answer concerning my complaint. And the Lord answered me, and said, Write the vision and make it plain upon tables, that he may run that readeth it. For the vision is yet for the appointed time, and it hasteth towards the end, and shall not lie: though it tarry, wait for it; because it will surely come, it will not delay.

Habakkuk's concern was with the moral problem presented by Yahweh's use of so cruel and inhuman a foe as Babylon for his purpose in bringing Judah to punishment for her sins. The prophecy in general has been characterized as 'the fruit of religious reflection',[1] and there are indications that some verses of chapter ii (apart from verses 1ff) are adapted from phrases in the earlier prophecies of Micah and Isaiah.[2] In view of these considerations, and in accordance with the understanding of Isa. xxi here presented, it is likely that Hab. ii 1f consciously reflects (the eighth-century form of) Isa. xxi 6ff.[3]

On this view of the relationship between the two texts it should be noted that Habakkuk is concerned by his use of the image of the watchman to express his patient expectation of Yahweh's answer to the problem that he faced. The answer was to be committed to writing in such a way that the reader would clearly and readily perceive its import, though its fulfilment was to be delayed until the appointed time.

In the light of this prophecy, it may be suggested that Isa. xxi 6ff was seen in the sixth century B.C. as a prophecy granted to Isaiah, the fulfilment of which was delayed until the present times. That there is no reference in Habakkuk to the detailed contents of the vision of Isa. xxi 6ff (i.e. to the terms רכב etc.) suggests

---

1 A. F. Kirkpatrick, *The Doctrine of the Prophets*, 3rd edn, (London, 1901), p. 273.
2 See S. R. Driver, *The Minor Prophets* (Century Bible) (Edinburgh, 1906), p. 59.
3 Wildberger explains the striking similarities between Hab. ii 1ff and Isa. xxi by assuming that the motif of the watchman was a customary way of understanding the prophetic office in prophetic circles. The possibility of any (literary) dependence is precluded for him because, of course, he attributes Isa. xxi to a date in the sixth century B.C.

that the important element in the original prophecy was thought in the sixth century to be the motif of the watchman (or prophet) whose function was patiently to await the fulfilment of Yahweh's words, however great the apparent delay.[1]

Whether the apparent distinction between the prophet (אלי) and the watchman (המצפה) was itself the object of sixth-century interpretation can be only a matter for conjecture. However, if the essential element was understood to be the inexorable fulfilment of prophecy, even after long delay (cf. verse 8), it is probable that the watchman was, in the eyes of the sixth-century interpreters, either one of themselves or even, perhaps, the prophet Habakkuk himself. (Cf. Rashi, p. 28 above.)

Verse 7

Eighth century

'*And when he sees*[a] *two-horse chariots*[b,2] . . .[c] *then he shall pay very great attention.*'

a. It is natural to suppose that verse 7 constitutes a continuation of the command of verse 6 (p. 30).

b. While it is reasonably certain that רכב at this earlier date denoted 'chariots' rather than 'riders' it is not certain whether a single chariot is meant or whether the word denotes collectively 'chariots'. However, while both usages are clearly attested (see B.D.B., p. 939), the balance of probability may be said to favour the latter view.

A number of biblical references refer to the might of Assyria in terms of her chariots (2 Kings xix 23 = Isa. xxxvii 24; Nahum ii 4, 5, 14); in particular Isa. xxii 7 makes use of an expression very similar to that used here in order to depict the eighth-century invasion of Judah by the Assyrian army. It may be assumed, therefore, that the prophet (or else the watchman)

---

1 Where Habakkuk is concerned it is even possible that his emphasis upon a clear written message represents a desire for elucidation of the obscurer elements in Isaiah's prophecy.

2 The accentuation of the M.T. is commonly emended so that the athnah is placed beneath the word פרשים; see e.g. B.H.[(3)] and Wildberger. Because the authenticity of the similar phrase in Isa. xxii 6 (רכב אדם פרשים) is questioned, I have not considered it as evidence here.

saw in his vision chariots and that chariots denoted for him the might of Assyria.[1]

c. The words רכב חמור רכב גמל are taken to be a later addition to the text; see below. Here it may be noted that the four words are not present in verse 9. There is no evidence that the term רכב was used to denote (baggage) wagons as opposed to chariots, and that camels and asses should have been employed to pull chariots is surely unthinkable (p. 32).

Sixth century

And he will see[a] *mounted cavalry* (רכב), *horsemen in pairs* (צמד פרשים,[b]) *men riding on asses, men riding on camels* (רכב חמור רכב גמל).[c] *And he will pay very great attention.*

a. Because now the prophecy is understood to concern the (contemporary) sixth-century fall of Babylon, the words are seen as a prediction (uttered by Isaiah). The watchman, now not Isaiah but a contemporary, will see what Yahweh had predicted to Isaiah that he (the watchman) would see.

b. It is likely that in the sixth century the word רכב was understood to denote mounted cavalry (cf. ibn Barun's philological explanation, p. 30 above) and that צמד פרשים was taken to mean pairs of horsemen (pp. 30ff). Such an interpretation of the words in question can be traced back at least as far as the LXX (pp. 30f above).

In this connexion it is suggested that the puzzling phrase רכב איש in verse 9 may be illuminated. If רכב was interpreted in the sixth century as (human) riders rather than as chariotry, that interpretation may have thereafter been fixed by the addition of the word איש as a gloss to the word רכב.[2]

On the view outlined above, readers of the sixth century would have found in these words a reference to cavalry and mounted troopers, a feature of warfare conspicuously associated with the Persians.[3]

c. The phrase רכב חמור רכב גמל cannot, it is submitted, mean anything other than riders on asses and camels. For this reason,

---

1 Cf. the reliefs of Tiglath-pileser III and Sennacherib displayed in public in the British Museum. Both are there depicted as occupying two-horse chariots.

2 Cf. D.B.D.'s observations on the phrase רכב אדם in Isa. xxii 6; here the LXX renders: ἀναβάται ἄνθρωποι. For Procksch's similar (but not identical) views, see pp. 34f above.

3 See p. 32 and Wiseman, *Peoples*, p. 335.

and in the light of the references in Herodotus and Xenophon (p. 64 above) to the use made by the Persians of asses and camels, it is here suggested that the phrase was inserted as a sixth-century *vaticinium ex eventu* designed to facilitate the use of the text as referring to the Persians.

Verses 8 and 9a

Eighth century

And he called out 'I was looking [a] *...* [b] *and, behold, there came*

a. The M.T.'s אריה is taken to be a corruption of an original אֶרְאֶה (see p. 34; so Marti). The verb, used in the imperfect to express continued action in the past (G.K. 107b), bears this meaning, as frequently, when used absolutely and followed by והנה (B.D.B., p. 907 6c). As Marti observes, the conjunction of the verb ראה with הנה provides precisely the form in which Zechariah introduces his visions (Zech. ii 1; iv 2; v 1, 9; vi 1). b. The words from על מצפה to the end of verse 8 are understood to be a later addition to the original text. With Marti two considerations may be advanced in support of the view that they form no part of the original text:

(1) The structure of the verse requires two, rather than three, two-beat parts; and to arrange it in the latter way would have the effect of spoiling the parallelism.[1]

(2) The sense of the narrative runs on better without the words (see above) and their presence in the oracle (with consequent corruption of the original text) can be explained by reference to later texts (see below).

Sixth century (verse 8)

And the seer [a] *cried: 'All day long I stand on the Lord's watchtower, and I am stationed every night upon my watch.'* [b]

a. The reading of 1QIs[a] is here adopted. On the present view of the oracle, the original reading אראה will have been modified in the sixth century to הראה[2] in order to accommodate the addition which follows. The reading provides a subject for the

---

1 Marti's second argument (viz. that the words are at odds with the content of verse 4) is not here reproduced because I take a different view of verse 4.

2 Goshen-Gottstein inclines to the view that the reading אריה gave rise to the reading הראה in 1QIs[a].

verb ויקרא, and the phrase ויקרא הראה ('and the seer cried') introduces the direct speech which follows it. The participial form הראה depicts the one looking out (i.e. the watchman), but it also describes his function as the receiver of a revelation from God (B.D.B., p. 906f (para. 1b)).

The reading of the M.T. אריה may be regarded as an early corruption of הראה[1] made either accidentally by scribal error or deliberately in order to provide a particular interpretation of the watchman's vision. In connexion with the second of these possibilities the reference may be made to the avenging wrath of Yahweh against his enemies (here Babylon), depicted under the figure of a lion; cf. Isa. xxxi 4; Jer. iv 7, xlix 19 = l 44.

b. The direct speech of the seer may be illuminated by reference to Hab. ii 1ff and to Isa. lxii 6. In the former text Habakkuk waits patiently at his prophetic station for the time when Yahweh will vouchsafe an answer to his problem. In Isa. lxii 6 watchmen, whether (as I think) prophets or angelic beings, are depicted as waiting constantly on Jerusalem's walls for the dawn of the day of salvation.

In the light of these two texts (which are verbally very similar to the direct speech of this verse) it may be assumed that Isaiah's original and somewhat simple motif of the watchman has been modified and interpreted in the sixth century by the addition of the words in direct speech. Thereby, the watchman becomes for the sixth century the later prophet (הראה) whose function is patiently to await and to expound the fulfilment of Yahweh's word in his own times.

On this understanding of the texts, the detailed relationship between them will be as follows:

The original text of Isa. xxi 6–8 is the source of the sixth-century motif (indicated by Hab. ii 1ff as well as by the later text of Isa. xxi) of the prophet as a watchman continually waiting for Yahweh's revelation). If Hab. ii 1ff is an echo of the original text of Isa. xxi 6ff then the later text of Isa. xxi 6ff reflects a similar sixth-century reinterpretation of that earlier text. Isa. lxii 6 is in turn a post-exilic[2] echo of the sixth-century

---

1 Alternatively, we may suppose that the original אראה was preserved in some older manuscripts which survived the sixth-century revision and it is this reading which lies behind the erroneous (or deliberate) reading אריה of the M.T.

2 For a date in the mid fifth century B.C., see Marti, pp. 389f.

texts (with their motif of the prophet as a watchman continually waiting for Yahweh's revelation). In Isa. lxii 6 the function of the watchmen (now plural) is to work and pray tirelessly for the restoration of Jerusalem.

Verse 9

Eighth century

'And behold, there came: two-horse chariots.' [a] *And he responded by saying:* [b] *'Fallen, fallen is Babylon and all the images of her gods are shattered to the ground.'* [c]

a. רכב צמד פרשים is regarded as the eighth-century text, the word איש being a sixth-century addition. See above on verse 6.
b. For ענה with אמר in the sense 'to respond to an occasion, to speak in view of circumstances', see B.D.B., p. 773 2a. The prophet, or watchman, himself responds to what he has seen by uttering his interpretation of it.
c. The reference to the shattering of the Babylonians' idols is unlikely to be a *vaticinium ex eventu.* Rather Isaiah saw the inevitability of Babylon's wholesale destruction at the hands of the Assyrians. That his estimate was accurate may be inferred from the events of 689 B.C., when Sennacherib actually invested Babylon and destroyed her gods (p. 109).

Sixth century

'And behold, there comes mounted cavalry, horsemen in pairs.' [a] *And he answered and said: 'Fallen, fallen is Babylon and all the images of her gods are shattered to the ground.'*

a. See on verse 7, eighth and sixth centuries (pp. 125ff).

As the prophet Isaiah is regarded as appointing a watchman who will await the fulfilment of his prophecy (cf. on verse 6 – sixth century), the subject of the verbs 'answered' and 'said' is most likely to be Isaiah himself. In other words, the prophecy is understood to mean 'When you (*sc.* the watchman of the future) see the sign of mounted cavalry, my prophecy "Fallen is Babylon" will be fulfilled.'

Evidence that the phrase 'Fallen is Babylon' was interpreted by reference to the sixth-century fall of Babylon may be deduced from the presence in Jer. li 8 of very similar words. Again, in

Jer. l 2 reference is made to the destruction of the Babylonian gods in language markcdly similar to that of Isa. xxi 9 (see p. 114).

Verse 10

Eighth century

O my people threshed[a] *and winnowed on my threshing-floor,*[b] *what I have heard from the LORD of hosts, the God of Israel, I have declared to you.*

a. Lit. 'my threshing'.
b. Lit. 'son of my threshing-floor, (see p. 38).

The metaphor is used proleptically of Judah's fate.[1] By becoming involved in foreign alliances, Judah was to incur the inevitable punishment of having to bear the ruthless oppression of Assyria. This is the message that Isaiah has learned in his vision and he recounts it to his hearers (cf. p. 112). The note of sympathy which characterizes the verse is in accord with the horror experienced by the prophet at the onset of his vision. Both feelings are experienced by the prophet by reason of his harsh vision (verse 2).

Sixth century

There is no discernible change to the text. The evidence of Jer. li 33 suggests that for the sixth century it was Babylon which was thought of as threshed and winnowed: 'The daughter of Babylon is like a threshing-floor at the time when it is trodden...' (R.V.). Yet the text with its sympathetic tone and its emphasis upon its being communicated by Yahweh to his people (לכם) suggests that for the sixth century, as for the eighth, it was Israel who was addressed as threshed and winnowed (cf. p. 39). We may suppose that for the later generation recollection of Zion's anguish prompted the expectation that the agents of that anguish would in their turn suffer it themselves (see p. 119).

1 If Mic. iv 13 (in which it is said that the daughter of Zion will thresh many nations) is quoted by Micah from the words of an eighth-century prophet of national well-being, then Isaiah like Micah may, by use of the metaphor, be deliberately seeking to reverse the arguments of such contemporary false prophets. For recent views on Mic. iv 11ff, see A. S. van der Woude in *V.T.*, 1969, pp. 252ff, Rudolph, *K.A.T.* XIII 3, p. 92, and Lindblom, *Prophecy in Ancient Israel* (Oxford, 1962), p. 251n.

4

Verses 11–17

History and exegesis

The impression gained by a number of scholars that the Dumah oracle and the Arabian oracles reflect the same general historical circumstances has been noted (pp. 91ff). By way of summary, three considerations may be advanced in support of this view: first, both are concerned with the geographical area to the south of Judah; secondly, they are both marked by similar dialectal features; thirdly, they are juxtaposed.[1]

Again arguments have been advanced above to suggest that the oracles pre-date the sixth century B.C.; in particular (pp. 93ff) there is evidence that the sixth-century Edom oracle of Jer. xlix 7ff knew and made use of Isaiah's (Arabian) oracle. Further (pp. 98f, 102), it is argued that the epilogues to the Moab oracles (cf. Isa. xvf) and to the Arabian oracle come from the same hand and derive from the sixth century; one of them (Isa. xvi 13) explicitly states that the material to which it is appended was 'the word that the Lord spake concerning Moab in time past'.

Finally, literary considerations and in particular comparison of the Moab oracles (Isa. xvf) with Isa. xxi 11ff suggested that these oracles reflect the period of the Assyrian attacks on southern Palestine and Arabia at the end of the eighth century B.C. (see pp. 98ff).

In order to gain further insights into the oracles of Isa. xxi 11ff it is necessary to turn again to the evidence provided by the sixth-century oracle of Jer. xlix 7ff. The evidence that the latter chapter affords is likely to be of a sort with that which Jer. lf yielded for the elucidation of Isa. xxi 1–10.

1. Jer. xlix 7ff is explicitly and clearly an oracle directed against Edom. It contains in verse 8a a summons to the

---

[1] The LXX has no title for verses 13ff and consequently appears to regard verses 11ff as one oracle (see p. 53).

131

inhabitants of Dedan to flee far off, apparently from Edom, in order to avoid the calamity which is about to fall upon that country. Although the verbs are not the same as those used in relation to the caravans of Dedanites in Isa. xxi 13[1] the meaning is clearly so similar that it is natural to assume that Jer. xlix 8a consciously reflects Isa. xxi 11ff in exactly the way that Jer. xlviii reflects Isa. xvf.[2]

From the considerations so far adduced I conclude that Jer. xlix 7ff constitutes evidence that the Dumah oracle was understood in the sixth century B.C. to be an oracle directed against Edom and not against the Arabian Dumah (Dumat al Jandal). Further, because there is within the oracle itself (Isa. xxi 11) a reference to Seir, often in the O.T. a synonym for Edom, and, because there is no evidence that the reference is a later addition or correction to an earlier reading (*contra* Lohmann; see p. 83 above), I further conclude that the oracle, as received by the author of Jer. xlix (and therefore originally), was an oracle directed against Edom (and not against Arabian Dumah). Secondly, because the Edom oracle of Jer. xlix contains *within itself* a reference to the Dedanites, it is possible to conclude that in the sixth century the Edom oracle of Isa. xxi 11 was understood to contain *within it* a reference to the Dedanites. In support of that conclusion there is the corroborative evidence of the LXX (see p. 53 above). Accordingly we may state that the Edom oracle of Isa. xxi 11ff was received in the sixth century as a single oracle which included references to the Dedanites, rather than as two separate oracles ('Dumah' and 'Arabia'). On the other hand, it is possible to argue that to the author of the Edom oracle of Jer. xlix *two* oracles of Isaiah ('Dumah' and 'Arabia') were so closely linked that he felt free to modify them in order to achieve for himself a single oracle against Edom which included reference to the Dedanites. The balance of probability may be held to swing in favour of the former conclusion in view of the further consideration that Jer. xlix 28ff contains oracles against Arab peoples (Kedar and Hazor); if

---

1 For the possibility that they do in fact reflect the verbs of Isa. xxi, see p. 139 below.

2 Rudolph (p. 281) has shown that the author of Jer. xlviii at times followed his older sources very closely and at others treated them with very considerable freedom. With this conclusion my estimate of the way in which Jer. lf has used Isa. xxi 1–10 seems to be consistent.

the author had wished to refer to earlier material concerning the Arabs, he would have been most likely to include it precisely here rather than within an oracle against Edom.[1]

2. The Edom oracle of Jer. xlix 7ff clearly reflects the hatred felt for Edom by the Jews after 587 B.C.[2] Such feelings are not characteristic of earlier prophecies against that country, and Jeremiah's original sayings about Edom, for example, do not display this attitude.[3] In the Edom oracle of Isa. xxi 11f there is no apparent trace of hatred; rather a sympathetic note has usually been detected (see pp. 75ff).

These considerations support the conclusion, reached on other grounds, that Isaiah's Edom oracle clearly antedates the sixth century B.C. On the other hand, it is likely that the oracle would have been the object of the sort of reinterpretation that has been suggested for the oracle of verses 1–10. It is suggested below that just such a reinterpretation may be detected, and that in particular it was achieved by creating out of the single Edom oracle two separate oracles – one concerning Edom and the other concerning Arabia.

3. The Edom oracle of Jer. xlix contains material which is common to that found in the sixth-century (anti-Edomite) prophecy of Obadiah. The balance of scholarly opinion may be said to favour the view that the two oracles are dependent upon a common source – whether that source was written or oral (see p. 93n).

Obad. 5f is clearly a variant form of what is found in Jer. xlix 9f. It is likely that Obadiah here preserves a better as well as an earlier form of the text, for, as Rudolph observes,[4] the text of Obad. 5 fits the general context well, whereas that of Jer. xlix 9 is in many respects unsatisfactory in the context.

---

1 That virtually the same verbs are used in relation to the inhabitants of Hazor (verse 30) as are used in verse 8 of the Dedanites is not here significant. The important point is that Dedanites are *not* mentioned within the Arabian oracle of Jer. xlix 28ff, whereas they are within the Edom oracle.

2 See e.g. Rudolph, pp. 291 ff; a particularly clear example is the use to which words originally used of Babylon (Jer. l 44–6) have been put in Jer. xlix 19–21. Now the fall of Edom rather than that of Babylon causes the whole world to tremble.

3 See Haller in *Z.A.W.* Bei. 41 (1925), 109ff, and Weiser, p. 407. Jer. xlix 22 may here be cited as an example of the factual as opposed to the gloating notices of Edom's discomfiture.

4 *K.A.T.* XIII 2, p. 297.

The Hebrew text of Obad. 5 runs:

אם גנבים באו לך (אם שודדי לילה איך נדמיתה) הלוא יגנבו דים

אם בצרים באו לך הלוא ישאירו עוללות

‎(6)‏ איך נחפשו עשו נבעו מצפניו

B.H.[3] followed by Wolff is inclined to the view that the words between the brackets, being absent in Jer. xlix 9, are a gloss. On the other hand Rudolph does not take this view, and, by inverting the order of the phrases underlined, he is able to restore the text adequately. Against the view of B.H.[3] and Wolff, it should be noted that the word לילה occurs also in the text of Jer. xlix 9 (though here after the word גנבים). This, understood in association with the impression reached by comparing the two texts, suggests that here as elsewhere we are likely to be concerned with a variant text rather than with a gloss.

The Hebrew text may be rendered (after the R.V. but following Rudolph's rearrangement):

> If thieves came to thee, if robbers by night, would they
> not steal till they had enough? How art thou cut off!
> If grape-gatherers came to thee, they would not leave
> gleaning grapes![1] How are the things of Esau searched
> out! How are his hidden treasures sought up!

In this passage there are three Hebrew words (overlined) which are found in the Dumah oracle of Isaiah, viz. לילה נדמיתה, (cf. דומה in Isa. xxi 11) and most important, the verb נבעו from the root בעה (cf. תבעיון בעיו). Similarly, Obad. 5 and the repeated words of lament in Isa. xv 1 have three words in common. Isa. xv 1 runs: כי בליל שדד ער מואב נדמה.

A comparison then of the three texts suggests the following conclusions: Obad. 5f (cf. Jer. xlix 9f) reflects the Dumah oracle of Isa. xxi and at least the first verse of the Moab oracle of Isa. xvf.[2] That it reflects specifically the Dumah oracle is likely in view of the fact that both use the word בעה in apparently the same way. Further, this interpretation is consistent with

---

1 Reading לא for הלא with Jer. xlix; cf. Rudolph's slightly different treatment.
2 The mention of grape-gatherers etc. may be a free reflection of the mention in Isa. xvi 8ff. of the spoiling of Moab's vines.

the fact that Jer. xlix 8, another form of the same *Vorlage*, shows knowledge of Isa. xxi 13 (and probably 12b – see below).

Because the *Vorlage* of Obad. 5f and Jer. xlix appears to know both Isa. xv 1 and the Dumah oracle and because the latter texts contain two words in common, viz. ליל(ה) and forms of the root דמה, I infer that the Moab oracle and the Dumah oracle are of a sort and that the former may be used to illuminate the latter. With this inference the considerations set out above (pp. 98ff) are consistent: the two texts seem to derive from Assyrian times when Moab, Edom (and Arabia) were objects of Assyrian aggression and were shown at least a modicum of sympathy by the Judaean prophet. There is no reason to suppose otherwise than that the prophet was Isaiah ben Amoz.

On this view of the text, Isaiah's Edom oracle is likely to come from the same time as his oracle concerning Babylon (verses 1–10), i.e. during the last years of the eighth century B.C. In this connexion it may be recalled that both Edom and Moab were tributary to Tiglath-pileser III in 724 (*A.N.E.T.*, p. 282). In 713 Edom and Moab were drawn into the revolt against Sargon led by Ashdod (Luckenbill, II, no. 195). The Assyrian king invested Ashdod and Gath (*C.A.H.*, III, p. 58) and, as a consequence, Moab and Edom paid tribute and thus avoided invasion themselves.

The death of Sargon in 705 B.C. was the cause of widespread revolt in Syria–Palestine, and Hezekiah of Judah was one of the principal conspirators. Sennacherib's campaign of 701–700 was directed against this rebellion in which Edom and Moab clearly played a part. In common with certain other lesser conspirators, they seem to have paid (heavy) tribute and consequently yet again they avoided suffering an Assyrian invasion (Luckenbill, II, no. 239; cf. *C.A.H.*, III, p. 72).

A Hebrew ostracon recently discovered at Arad[1] and dated 701 B.C. appears to be concerned with communications between Edom and the king of Judah during the time of Sennacherib's campaign. Unfortunately the text is too fragmentary to throw any very particular light on the history of the time or upon the text of Isaiah. On the other hand, it is interesting that the name

---

1 See Aharoni.

'Edom' occurs no less than three times in the text and explicitly alongside mention of the king of Judah. We may conclude that communication with Edom was of some importance to Judah and to Hezekiah and that for Isaiah to have delivered an oracle concerned with Edom was in keeping with his having delivered oracles concerned with the other nations involved in the rebellion against Assyria.

If Isaiah's Edom oracle has been correctly dated in the closing years of the eighth century, then it is not to be regarded as a *vaticinium ex eventu*. Rather, like the Babylon oracle of verses 1–10 it sets forth by way of warning the consequences of involvement in the anti-Assyrian conspiracy. The description of fugitives fleeing from Edom to Arabia before the vehemence of war is sufficiently general to imply that the author was able to imagine the consequences of rebellion. The cipher of the watchman, on the other hand, seems to reflect a particular aspect of relations between Edom and Judah, probably their mutual involvement in the planning of rebellion (see below).

Comparison has been made between the Moab oracles of Isa. xvf and Isaiah's Edom oracle (see pp. 98ff) and on the basis of it the suggestion was made, albeit tentatively, that both oracles belong to the Assyrian period. It has recently been suggested that the core of the Moab oracles[1] is based upon earlier non-Isaianic laments over Moab occasioned by such attacks upon her as those perpetrated by the 'men of Gidir land'.[2] The latter are thought to be connected with the semi-nomads east of Moab in the latter part of the eighth century. It is not possible here to attempt a full evaluation of the Moab oracles; but if this assessment of one of them is correct there is no reason why Isaiah should not have used and redirected them to convey his message of warning in the period of the revolt following Sargon's death in 705.[3]

1 See esp. xv 1–8 and xvi 6–11.

2 For the source of our knowledge of this attack, see H. W. F. Saggs, 'The Nimrud Letters, 1952 – Part II', *Iraq* 17 (1955), 126–60. See also Wildberger, pp. 597, 606ff, and Wiseman, *Peoples*, p. 239.

3 For this sort of approach, see e.g. the admirably cautious and balanced statement of W. Rudolph, *H.S.S.* Wildberger's contention (p. 604) that no pre-exilic prophet ever cited and commented upon earlier oracles (and that consequently Isaiah could not have done so here) is somewhat dogmatic. As Rudolph observes, if Isaiah preached the imminent fulfilment of older oracles, that does not require that he identified himself with all their contents, nor does it necessarily detract from his general originality and greatness.

In the Edom oracle the metaphor of the watchman was, as Lohmann has indicated (pp. 83ff above), probably taken over by Isaiah from everyday life and used (probably as a cipher) to present his particular message concerning Edom.[1] Similar appropriation may be seen in, for example, the use made by Isaiah (v 1–7) of the song of the vineyard or (by a later prophet in xxiii 16) of the harlot's song.

Translation and commentary

Verse 11

Eighth century

Oracle concerning Dumah.[a] *They call*[b] *to me from Seir, 'Watchman',*[c] either '*what news of the night? Watchman, what news of the night?*' or[d] '*How much of the night remains? Watchman, how much of the night remains?*'

It is assumed that the image of the city watchman (p. 43) who replies ostensibly to a question concerning the night constitutes a cipher by which the prophet refers to the historical situation. There is no need to assume that the oracle is other than a contrived or imaginary prophetic vision, though the anti-Assyrian alliance of Hezekiah's time presumably necessitated communication between Edom and Judah.[2] The speech is purposely dialectal and the language evoked is likely to be Edomite or (international) Aramaic.[3]

a. משה דומה is read. The term Dumah denotes 'ruin, destruction' and is used proleptically of the fate which Isaiah believes will or may befall Edom if she persists in her rebellion against Assyria (אם תבעיון). The word is to be derived from the root דמה[4] and reflects the use to which the word is put in Isa. xv 1, viz. that Ar (or Kir or Moab)[5] is destroyed, ruined on the night of *šdd*. On the other hand, its form and sound are evocative of

---

1 I am not committed, of course, to Lohmann's detailed conclusions.
2 Cf. the contents of the Arad ostracon of 701 B.C. (pp. 135f above).
3 See above, p. 79.
4 B.D.B., p. 198; see further G. R. Driver, 'A Confused Hebrew Root' in ספר טור־סיני (Jerusalem, 1960).
5 For the different views taken of the syntax of the line, see the standard commentaries.

the word Edom (אדום).[1] The use of the word דומה to denote Edom may be compared with Isaiah's use of the term גיא חזיון in chapter xxii to denote Jerusalem and especially if, as Driver supposes, the word is here cognate with Arabic *ḥzy* and denotes 'valley of calamity'.

b. Lit. '(Someone) is calling.' The participle is understood to have an impersonal force. Cf. with Delitzsch xxx 24, xxxiii 4 and Luther's translation: 'man ruft'.

c. The watchman (שמר) is Isaiah and the term may be regarded as similar to the prophet's description of himself as מצפה (watchman) in the previous oracle. His use here of the term is an accommodation to the nature of the oracle as a cipher.

d. For these alternative ways of understanding the question, see pp. 43ff. The question refers to the night, a symbol of Assyrian oppression. More particularly, it is suggested that the night is the ליל שדד of Isa. xv 1 (cf. Obad. 5), the night of the שֹׁדֵד (*sic* – the word is pointed שֻׁדַּד in Isa. xv 1), and that שֹׁדֵד denotes, as in Isa. xxi 2, the Assyrian devastator. The further question whether the night is an image of general Assyrian oppression or a particular historical example of that oppression cannot be answered with certainty. The repeated question of the Edomites portrays (however precisely it is understood) their longing for the morning of freedom from Assyrian domination.

Verse 12

Eighth century

The watchman said: 'If morning has come, then so has night.[a] *If you are involved in aggression then you will be the object of aggression.'*[b]

a. For simple perfects (here a perfect and an implied perfect – וְגַם) in a conditional sentence, G.K. 159h. This understanding yields a better sense than the rather dull and straightforward 'Morning has come and with it night.'

The morning is taken to mean the opposite of the night of oppression referred to in the question. Whether it denotes

---

1 Cf. e.g. the spelling of the word in the Assyrian texts *udumu* and in the LXX Ιδουμαια.

generally longed-for freedom or whether a particular historical attempt to achieve freedom cannot now be known.[1]

b. For the M.T.'s בְּעָיוֹ a pual imperative form is read: בָּעְיוּ. The imperative conveys a 'distinct assurance or threat' (G.K. 110c). For a discussion of the verb בעה, see pp. 48ff. It was there suggested that the word had a military or hostile connotation and it was noted that in Obad. 6 the niphal of the verb meant that Edom's wealth was exposed and plundered. The particular sense required in this context where no object is provided for the active verb is 'aggressive (military) action'.

The active verb 'If you are involved in aggression' is seen to match the longed-for 'day' and the passive 'you will be the object of aggression' matches the menacing וגם לילה 'then so has night'.

Verse 13

Eighth century

Turn back, go into the scrub; you must stay[2] amongst the Arabs.

The verbs שובו אתיו which in the M.T. form the end of verse 12 are taken with the words ביער בערב which in the M.T. form the beginning of the Arabian oracles. In Jer. xlix 8, where the Dedanites are summoned to flight, the two verbs employed are נֻסוּ הָפְנוּ. The latter verb is usually regarded as a hophal imperative of the verb פנה with the sense 'be ye turned back'.[3] It is at once apparent that the word is virtually synonymous with the verb שובו used in the phrase שובו אתיו in Isa. xxi 12, and we may conclude that here as elsewhere Jer. xlix reflects Isa. xxi. Indeed, the phrase נֻסוּ הָפְנוּ may constitute a rendering of the dialectal phrase שובו אתיו. At any rate Jer. xlix 8 is an indication that the words שובו אתיו denote flight and that they belong with what follows them rather than (as in the M.T.) with what precedes them.

The title משא בערב is understood to be a sixth-century (or later) addition to the text (see below). A consequence of this

1 If the latter meaning is the correct one, it is tempting, but probably fanciful, to see in the Arad ostracon (pp. 135f above) a reference to the Day of Freedom; line 11 contains the phrase *rd ym* and Aharoni, comparing Judg. xix 11, has suggested that the phrase may denote the passing (lit. 'going down') of a day.
2 For the use of the jussive to convey advice, see G.K. 109 b.
3 B.D.B., pp. 815f; cf. G.K. 46a.N.

understanding of the text is that parallelism is restored to verse 14 (see above, pp. 57f, and below).

The verse as restored and translated above forms the next part of Isaiah's Edom oracle. As a result of their rebellious activities, the Edomites will be reduced to fleeing their country for the safety of Arabia, just as the Moabites in Isa. xv 4ff are obliged to flee to Edom. Some echo of this form of the text may be detected in Obad. 7 where Edomites are spoken of as being 'driven out to their border'.[1]

Verse 14

Eighth century

O caravans of Dedanites, bring water to meet the thirsty; O inhabitants of the land of Teima, meet[a] the fugitives with food.

a. The pointing is emended so that an imperative form is read. The requirements of parallelism suggest that in the original text the caravans of Dedanites, like the inhabitants of Teima, were urged to show compassionate hospitality to the Edomite refugees. It is suggested below that in the sixth century B.C. the Dedanites themselves were understood to be the refugees to whom the inhabitants of Teima (and others) were urged to bring sustenance, and consequently a separate oracle (בערב ? 'Against the Arabs') was formed. Apart from the argument concerning parallelism, we may note that in Ezekiel's Edom oracle (xxv 12ff) it is said that Edom's desolation will stretch from Teman 'even unto Dedan' (R.V.); it is possible that this sixth-century text (see Zimmerli, pp. 588ff), in which Dedan is mentioned as a far-off place where Edomite refugees fall by the sword, preserves an echo of the original text of Isa. xxi 14, where Dedanites, so far from fleeing themselves, represented shelter to which refugees from Edom had recourse.

Against the view that the Dedanites were, in the original context of Isa. xxi 13ff, pictured as themselves refugees is the consideration that it would be curious to advise Dedanite

---

1 It should here be noted that the preceding verse is that which contains a form of the verb בעה (see above), and that the second part of Obad. 7 contains a reference to bread (cf. Isa. xxi 14); that the wording and content of Obad. 7b differs considerably from Isa. xxi 14 does not necessarily tell against literary dependence (see above).

caravans to lodge where they were accustomed to travel and presumably to lodge viz. among the nomadic peoples of North Arabia (בערב).

Verse 15

Eighth century

For they flee from the sword, from the strung bow and from the vehemence of war.

The verse states the reason for the flight of the Edomite refugees from their homeland into Arabia.

Sixth century (verses 11–15)

The evidence of Jer. xlix was understood to indicate that the text of Isaiah which it reflects contained a single oracle against Edom in which there was mention of the Dedanites (pp. 132ff). Secondly, the absence from Isa. xxi 11ff of the customary anti-Edomite polemic was noted.

When Isaiah's Edom oracle was received and interpreted in the sixth century, it is likely that it was understood in the light of the prevailing attitudes and of more recent historical events. All the sixth-century Edom prophecies which we have are marked by uncompromising hatred for Edom on the part of the Jews. As is well known, this attitude seems to have become prevalent shortly after 587 and the fall of Jerusalem.[1]

The evidence of Jer. xlixff suggests that Nebuchadrezzar's campaign against Judah's neighbours (599–587) made a very considerable impression on the Jews. In the course of those campaigns Nebuchadrezzar's army is known to have marched into the desert and plundered the Arabs.[2] It is possible that Edom was not left unscathed by such operations. In any case Edom was besieged by the later Babylonian king Nabonidus in the course of his march into Arabia in 554.[3]

1 For recent evaluations by Bartlett of Edom's role in the events leading up to the fall of Jerusalem, see Wiseman, *Peoples*, pp. 241f, and Bartlett, 'From Edomites to Nabataeans', p. 27n28.
2 In 599–598 according to Wiseman, *Chronicles*, p. 70; with this notice, Josephus's mention of an Arabian campaign should be compared; see above, p. 92.
3 *C.A.H.*, III, p. 405. For further references to the debate concerning the identification of 'Adummu', see p. 89n above. Lindsay, followed by Bartlett ('From Edomites to Nabataeans'), argues that it was this campaign which brought an end to the Edomite kingdom as such.

It is now suggested that in the sixth century B.C. Isaiah's Edom oracle (received initially as *one* oracle) was understood in the light of the Babylonian attacks upon Arabia and Edom of the first half of that century. In that the prophecy was seen already to reflect recent history, its words could be taken to form the basis for new prophecies of the longed-for total destruction of Edom (e.g. Jer. xlix).

In support of the conclusion that Isaiah's words were taken to refer *both* to Edom *and* to the Arabs, it should be noted that the sixth-century Jer. xlix 8 contains a summons to the Dedanites to flee from Edom in order to avoid imminent and certain calamity. Jer. xlix 30 contains virtually the same summons, but this time it is addressed to the inhabitants of (Arabian) Hazor and explicitly forms part of an oracle concerned with Nebuchadrezzar's attack upon the Arabs (and in particular upon Kedar). Thus, Jer. xlix indicates that words derived ultimately from Isa. xxi 11ff were later used *both* in an oracle concerned with Edom *and* in one concerned with Arabs.

The mode in which Isaiah's oracle was itself similarly reinterpreted may be reconstructed as follows: first, the vocative 'caravans of Dedanites' was construed not with the verb that follows it (התיו מים) but with the jussive and imperatives that precede it (תליו and שובו אתיו – see below). The effect was to initiate the creation of a separate oracle concerned with the Arabs. To have understood the text in this way (with Dedanite rather than Edomite refugees) would have precluded the detection in the sixth century of the sentiment of sympathy towards Edomite refugees, a sentiment which would ill accord with the vengeful spirit concerning Edom typical of the oracles of the time. Secondly, at this time, the supplementary material concerning Kedar (verses 16f) was added. Thirdly, and probably at a later stage, the title משא בערב was added to the text, but in such a way that it separated the phrase שובו אתיו from its proper place,[1] and caused it to be included in the watchman's reply of the Dumah oracle.

Only the smallest traces of the Dumah oracle are to be found in such sixth-century texts as Obadiah and Jer. xlix. In particular there appears to be no reference to the metaphor of the

---

[1] That Jer. xlix 8 preserves traces of the earlier way of construing the phrase has been noted above.

watchman and his questioners. It is therefore not possible to attempt a reconstruction of its detailed interpretation at this time. Indeed, perhaps its very obscurity and particularity precluded detailed reinterpretation. On the other hand, it seems clear that certain of its words and phrases were adopted in sixth-century oracles concerning Edom. These may be listed:

1. דומה. See Obad. 5 where it is said of Edom אֵיךְ נִדְמֵיתָ 'How art thou destroyed!'
2. (ה)ליל. See Obad. 5 (cf. Jer. xlix 9) where the phrase שודדי לילה is used in a metaphor whose purpose is to describe the total destruction of Edom.
3. אם תבעין בעיו. See Obad. 6. Here Edom's hidden treasures are ransacked (נבעו מצפניו).

The use of these phrases suggests that the Dumah oracle was, in the sixth century, thought to be consistent with the familiar message of Edom's (justified) destruction.

(Oracle concerning the Arabs)

Turn back, go into the scrub;[a] *amongst the Arabs you must stay, O caravans of Dedanites. (14) Bring water to meet the thirsty; O inhabitants of the land of Teima, meet*[b] *the fugitives with food. (15) For they flee from the sword, from the sharpened sword (or from the ubiquitous sword), from the strung bow and from the vehemence of war. (16) For the Lord has spoken to me thus: In a year, measured exactly (lit. as the years of a hireling),*[c] *all the might of Kedar shall be at an end. (17) And there will remain but a very few of the bowmen of the warriors of Kedar. The LORD the God of Israel has spoken.*

a. Jer. xlix 8 suggests, as we have seen, that שובו אתיו were in the sixth century construed with the Dedanites. At some stage after the composition of Jer. xlix a redactor added the title משא בערב, inserting it after the word אתיו and before the word ביער.
b. קַדְּמוּ. Piel imperative is read, as in the eighth-century text.
c. It is no longer possible to determine the circumstances which gave rise to this precise chronological statement; cf. Rudolph, *H.S.S.*, p. 142.

Principal Works Consulted

(Works which are cited only once are not included)

1 Hebrew or massoretic text

Biblia Hebraica, 3rd edn, ed. R. Kittel (Stuttgart, 1937).
Biblia Hebraica Stuttgartensia, ed. D. W. Thomas (Stuttgart, 1968).
The Book of Isaiah (The Hebrew University Bible), ed. M. H. Goshen-Gottstein (Jerusalem, 1975).

2 The ancient versions

The Peshitta. *Vetus Testamentum Syriace*, ed. S. Lee (London, 1823). See also Diettrich in sect. 7 below.
The Septuagint. *Septuaginta: Vetus Testamentum Graecum*, vol. XIV, *Isaias*, ed. J. Ziegler (Göttingen, 1939). See also Seeligmann and Ziegler in sect. 7 below.
The Targum. *The Targum of Isaiah*, ed. J. F. Stenning (Oxford, 1949).
The versions of Aquila, Synmmachus and Theodotion. *Origenis Hexaplorum quae supersunt*, ed. F. Field, vol. II (Oxford, 1875).
The Vulgate (sometimes referred to as 'Jerome'). *Biblia Sacra iuxta Vulgatam Versionem*, ed. R. Weber *et al.* (Stuttgart, 1969).

3 Lexica and dictionaries

Belot, J. B. *Vocabulaire arab–français* (Beyrouth, 1896).
Brockelmann, C. *Lexicon Syriacum* (Edinburgh and Berlin, 1895).
Brown, F., Driver, S. R. and Briggs, C. A. *A Hebrew and English Lexicon of the Old Testament* (Oxford, 1907).
Dozy, R. P. A. *Supplément aux dictionaires arabes* (Leiden, 1877).
Gesenius, W. and Buhl, F. *Handwörterbuch über das A.T.*, 16th edn (Leipzig, 1915).

Jastrow, M. *Dictionary of the Targumim, the Talmud Babli and Yerushalmi, and the Midrashic Literature* (2 vols., London, New York and Leipzig, 1886–1903).

Hoftijzer, J. *Dictionnaire des inscriptions sémitiques de l'Ouest* (Leiden, 1960).

Koehler, L. and Baumgartner, W. *Lexicon in Veteris Testamenti Libros* (Leiden, 1953). Cited as K.B.

Hebraïsches und Aramaïsches Lexikon zum Alten Testament, 3rd edn, ed. W. Baumgartner, B. Hartmann and E. Y. Kutscher, vol. I (Leiden, 1967), vol. II (Leiden, 1974). Cited as K.B.[3]

Lane, E. W. *Arabic–English Lexicon* (London, 1863–85).

Liddell, H. G. and Scott, R. *A Greek–English Lexicon*, rev. H. S. Jones (Oxford, 1940).

Payne Smith, R. *Thesaurus Syriacus* (Oxford, 1879–1901).

Wehr, H. *A Dictionary of Modern Written Arabic*, rev. J. M. Cowan (Wiesbaden and London, 1971).

4 Rabbinical commentators and authorities

Ben Bilam (11th century). J. Derenbourg (ed.), *Gloses d'Abou Zakariya Yahia Ben Bilam sur Isaïe* (Paris, 1892).

Ibn Barun (11th–12th centuries). P. Wechter (ed.), *Ibn Barun's Arabic Works on Hebrew Grammar and Lexicography* (Philadelphia, 1964).

Ibn Ezra (11th–12th centuries). M. Friedländer (ed.), *The Commentary of Ibn Ezra on Isaiah* (3 vols., London, 1873–7).

Ibn Janah (10th–11th centuries). A Neubauer (ed.), *The Book of Hebrew Roots* (Oxford, 1875).

Qimhi (12th–13th centuries). J. Levensohn (ed.), מקראות גדולות, vol. IX (Warsaw, 1866).

Rashi (11th–12th centuries). J. Levensohn (ed.), *ibid*.

Saadya (9th–10th centuries). J. Derenbourg (ed.), *R. Saadya ben Josef Al-Fayyoumi*, vol. III (Paris, 1896).

5 Commentaries on Isaiah

Bright, J. *Peake's Commentary on the Bible*, ed. M. Black and H. H. Rowley (London, 1963).

Cheyne, T. K. *The Prophecies of Isaiah*, vol. I (London, 1889). Cited as Cheyne, *P.I.*

Introduction to the Book of Isaiah (London, 1895). Cited as
    Cheyne, *I.B.I.*

Delitzsch, F. *Biblischer Commentar über den Propheten Jesaia*
    (Leipzig, 1866). Cited as Delitzsch (1) where it is necessary
    to distinguish between it and the 4th edn.

  The Prophecies of Isaiah, E. T. of Delitzsch (1) by J. Martin,
    vol. 1 (Edinburgh, 1877).

  Commentar über Das Buch Jesaia, 4th edn. (Leipzig, 1889).

  Biblical Commentary on the Prophecies of Isaiah, E.T. of the 4th
    edn by various translators, vol. 1 (Edinburgh, 1890).

Dillmann, C. F. A. *Der Prophet Jesaja*, 5th edn (Leipzig, 1890).
    Cited as Dillmann.

Dillmann, C. F. A. and Kittel, R. *Der Prophet Jesaja*, 6th edn
    (Leipzig, 1898). Cited as D.K.

Duhm, B. *Das Buch Jesaja*, 5th edn (Göttingen, 1968).

Ewald, H. *Die Propheten des Alten Bundes*, vol. 1, 2nd edn.
    (Göttingen, 1877).

Fohrer, G. *Das Buch Jesaja*, vol. 1 (Stuttgart and Zurich,
    1960).

Gray, G. B. *The Book of Isaiah (I–XXXIX)* (Edinburgh, 1912).

Hitzig, F. *Der Prophet Jesaja* (Heidelberg, 1833).

Kaiser, O. *Der Prophet Jesaja (13–39)* (Göttingen, 1973).
  Isaiah 13–39, E.T. by R. A. Wilson (London, 1974).

Kissane, E. J. *The Book of Isaiah*, vol. 1 (Dublin, 1960).

Lowth, R. *Isaiah* (London, 1778).

Marti, K. *Das Buch Jesaja* (Tübingen, 1900).

Migne, J.-P. *Patrologiae Latinae*, vol. XXIV (Hieronymus iv)
    (Paris, 1865).

Procksch, O. *Jesaja*, vol. 1 (chs. 1–39) (Leipzig, 1930).

Rosenmüller, E. F. C. *Scholia in Vetus Testamentum*, vol. III, no. 2
    (Leipzig, 1793).

Vitringa, C. *Commentarius in librum prophetiarum Jesaiae* (Leeu-
    warden, 1724).

Wildberger, H. *Biblischer Kommentar Altes Testament: Jesaja
    (13–22)*, vol. X, fasc. 2 (Neukirchen, 1974–7).

6 Modern commentaries on other O.T. prophets

Bright, J. *Jeremiah* (Anchor Bible) (Garden City, N.Y., 1965).

Duhm, B. *Das Buch Jeremia* (Tübingen and Leipzig, 1907).

Rudolph, W. *Jeremia*, 3rd edn. (Tübingen, 1968).

Joel, Amos, Obadja, Jona (Gütersloh, 1971). Cited as *K.A.T.* XIII 2.

Micha, Nahum, Habakuk, Zephanja (Gütersloh, 1975). Cited as *K.A.T.* XIII 3.

Ruth, Hohes Lied, Klagelieder (Gütersloh, 1962). Cited as *K.A.T.* XVII.

Volz, P. *Der Prophet Jeremia* (Leipzig and Erlangen, 1922).

Weiser, A. *Das Buch Jeremia* (chs. 25, 15–52, 34) (Das Alt Testament Deutsch, 21) (Göttingen, 1966).

Wolff, H. W. *Dodekapropheten*, vol. III. *Obadja und Jona* (Neukirchen, 1977).

Zimmerli, W. *Ezechiel*, vol. II (chs. 25–48) (Neukirchen, 1969).

7 Other works cited

Aharoni, Y. 'Three Hebrew Ostraca from Arad'. *B.A.S.O.R.* 197 (1970), 16–42 (esp. 28–32).

Ap-Thomas, D. R. 'All the King's Horses'. In J. I. Durham and J. R. Porter (eds.), *Proclamation and Presence: Essays in Honour of G. H. Davies* (London, 1970).

Bach, R. *Die Aufforderungen zur Flucht und zum Kampf in alttestamentlichen Prophetenspruch* (Neukirchen, 1962).

Barnes, W. 'A Fresh Interpretation of Isaiah xxi 1–10'. *J.T.S.* I (1900), 583–92.

Bartlett, J. R. 'The Moabites and Edomites'. In Wiseman (ed.), *Peoples*, pp. 229–58.

'From Edomites to Nabateans'. *P.E.Q.*, 1979, 53ff.

Baumgartner. See Koehler and Baumgartner, *Hebräisches*, in sect. 3 above.

Boutflower, C. 'Isaiah xxi in the Light of Assyrian History'. *J.T.S.* 14 (1913), 501–15.

Branden, A. van den. *Inscriptions thamoudéenes* (Louvain, 1950).

Brinkman, J. A. 'Elamite Military Aid to Merodach-Baladan'. *J.N.E.S.* 24 (1965), 161–6.

Buhl, F. 'Jesaja 21, 6–10'. *Z.A.W.* 8 (1888), 157–64.

Cambridge Ancient History, The, vol. III. *The Assyrian Empire*, ed. J. B. Bury, S. A. Cook and F. E. Adcock, 1st edn (Cambridge, 1925). Cited as *C.A.H.*, III.

Vol. iv. *The Persian Empire and the West*, ed. J. B. Bury, S. A. Cook and F. E. Adcock, 1st edn (Cambridge, 1926). Cited as *C.A.H.*, iv.

Cobb, W. H. 'Isaiah xxi. 1–10 Reexamined'. *J.B.L.* 17 (1898), 40–61.

Derenbourg, J. See in sect. 4 above (Ben Bilam and Saadya).

Dhorme, P. 'Le désert de la mer (Isaie XXI)'. *R.B.* 31 (1922), 403–6.

Diettrich, G. *Ein Apparatus criticus zur Pešitto zum Propheten Jesaia* (*Z.A.W.* Bei. 8, Giessen, 1905).

Donner, H. and Röllig, W. *Kannaanaïsche und aramaïsche Inschriften*, 3 vols. (Wiesbaden, 1962–4).

Driver, G. R. 'Isaiah I–XXXIX: Textual and Linguistic Problems'. *J.S.S.* 13 (1968), 46f.

Ehrlich, A.B. *Randglossen zur hebraïschen Bibel*, vol. iv (Leipzig, 1912).

Eitan, I. 'A contribution to Isaiah Exegesis'. *H.U.C.A.* 12–13 (1937–8), 55–88.

Erlandsson, S. *The Burden of Babylon* (Lund, 1970).

Fohrer, G. *Einleitung in das Alte Testament* (Heidelberg, 1965). Cited as Fohrer, *Einleitung*.

Friedländer, M. See in sect. 4 above (Ibn Ezra).

Gadd, C. J. 'The Harran Inscriptions of Nabonidus'. *Anatolian Studies. Journal of the British Institute of Archaeology at Ankara* 8 (1958), 35–92.

Galling, K. 'Jesaja 21 im Lichte der neuen Nabonidtexte'. In *Tradition und Situation: Festschrift A. Weiser* (Göttingen, 1963), pp. 49–62.

Gesenius–Kautzsch. *Gesenius' Hebrew Grammar*, 2nd English edn., rev. A. E. Cowley (Oxford, 1910).

Goshen-Gottstein. See in sect. 1 above.

Grätz, H. *Emendationes in Plerosque V.T. Libros* (Breslau, 1892–4).

Jamme, A. *Sabaean Inscriptions from Maḥram Bilqis* (Baltimore, Md., 1962).

Kleinert, P. 'Bemerkungen zu Jes. 20–22'. *Th.St.Kr.* 1 (1877), 174–9.

Lehman, I. O. 'A Forgotten Principle of Biblical Textual Tradition Rediscovered'. *J.N.E.S.* 26 (1967), 96f.

Lindsay, J. 'The Babylonian Kings and Edom, 605–550 B.C.'
    P.E.Q., 1976, pp. 23–39.

Lohmann, P. 'Das Wächterlied Jes. 21. 11, 12'. *Z.A.W.* 33
    (1913), 20–9.

Luckenbill, D. D. *Ancient Records of Assyria and Babylonia*, vol. II
    (Chicago, 1927).

Michaelis, J. D. *Supplementa ad Lexica Hebraica* (Göttingen,
    1792).

Möhle, A. *Mitteilungen des Septuaginta-Unternehmens* (*Theodoret zu
    Jesaia*) (Berlin, 1932), p. 88.

Naveh, J. 'Hebrew Texts in Aramaic script in the Persian
    Period?' *B.A.S.O.R.* 203 (1971), 27–32.

Neubauer, A. See in sect. 4 above (Ibn Janah).

Obermann, J. 'Yahweh's Victory over the Babylonian
    Pantheon'. *J.B.L.* 48 (1929), 307–28.

Ottley, R. R. *The Book of Isaiah According to the Septuagint*
    (Cambridge, 1906).

Otzen, B. *Studien über Deuterosacharja* (Copenhagen, 1964).

Pritchard J. B. *Ancient Near Eastern Texts Relating to the Old
    Testament* (Princeton, N.J., 1950). Cited as *A.N.E.T.*

Rabin, C. 'An Arabic Phrase in Isaiah'. In *Studi sull'Oriente e la
    Bibbia: Offerti a G. Rinaldi* (Genoa, 1967). Cited as Rabin,
    English.

עיונים בספר ישעיהו · א·, ed. B.-S. Loria (Jerusalem, 1976).
    Cited as Rabin, Hebrew.

Rudolph, W. 'Jesaja xv–xvi'. In D. W. Thomas and W. D.
    McHardy (eds.), *Hebrew and Semitic Studies Presented to G. R.
    Driver* (Oxford, 1963). Cited as Rudolph, *H.S.S.*

Schrader, E. *Die Keilinschriften und das A. T.*, 2nd edn (Giessen,
    1883).

Schwab, M. *Le Talmud de Jérusalem traduit*, vol. XVI (Paris,
    1883).

Scott, R. B. Y. 'Isaiah xxi 1–10: The Inside of a Prophet's
    Mind'. *V.T.* 2 (1952), 278–82.

Seeligmann, I. L. *The Septuagint Version of Isaiah: A Discussion of
    its Problems* (Leiden, 1948).

Stenning, J. F. See in sect. 2 above (Targum).

Talmud, The Palestinian. (יומא...מועד קטן) תלמוד ירושלמי
    (Zitomir, 1862).

Walton, B. *Biblia Sacra Polyglotta*, vol. III (London, 1657).

Wechter, P. See in sect. 4 above (Ibn Barun).

Wiseman, D. J. (ed.). *Chronicles of the Chaldean Kings* (London, 1956). Cited as Wiseman, *Chronicles*.

Wiseman, D. J. (ed.). *Peoples of O.T. Times* (Oxford, 1973). Cited as Wiseman, *Peoples*.

Ziegler, J. *Untersuchungen zur Septuaginta des Buches Isaias* (Münster, 1934). See also Septuagint in sect. 2 above.

Indexes

A. BIBLICAL REFERENCES
(References to Isaiah xxi are not listed)

B. GENERAL INDEX
(Authors of commentaries on biblical books are not included)

13/ Isa 33:1 In "expansion and reworking of" Isa 21:2 — so, commentaries.
   (ck)

Pt I "the text & its mng"
P.47–62
   — exhaustive compila & synthesis.
   — Mc. never translates panel so his plane
        reading is always a bit fuzzy

   · s.t. a pile-up of possibilities   95%
        w/c final determination.

pt II   "exegesis & Hist Bkgrd"
P. 63–102   weights all the hypotheses & suggestions
   see p 64.

Q what requires a dble reading?
        Diff versions?
        semantic ambiguity?